DIALOGUES
Philosopher meets Seer

Books by Swami Bodhananda

The Gita and Management

Rishi Vision

Meditation: the awakening of inner powers

Happiness Unlimited:
Self-Unfoldment in an Interactive World

DIALOGUES

Philosopher meets Seer

Sangeetha Menon

Swami Bodhananda

BLUEJAY BOOKS

An imprint of Srishti Publishers & Distributors

New Delhi & Calcutta

BLUEJAY BOOKS
An imprint of SRISHTI PUBLISHERS & DISTRIBUTORS
64-A, Adhchini
Sri Aurobindo Marg
New Delhi 110 017

First published in paper back by *BLUEJAY BOOKS* 2003
Paperback Edition published by *BLUEJAY BOOKS* 2003

ISBN 81-88575-01-1
Rs. 165.00

Cover painting: Nirmal Prakash
Cover design by
Creative Concept
40/223, C R Park
New Delhi 110 019

Typeset in JMJ_DiaTimes 13pt. by Skumar at Srishti

Printed and bound in India by
Saurabh Print-O-Pack, Noida

According to me, the main teaching of the *Gita* is to make work and relationships a means of self-exploration and self-expression.

SWAMI BODHANANDA

Contents

Contents

Introduction

Being trained as a philosopher and having a keen interest in 'consciousness' and 'mind' studies I am often confronted with questions that fall in the interface of real life situations and theoretical explanations for them. Trying to have a real life understanding of these issues, at the same time, without losing the philosophical rigour, I feel that, I often miss the crux of the story. Perhaps, what might be missing is a 'spiritual' point of view, a 'wisdom' point of view, a 'Seer's' point of view.

What is a Seer's point of view? I had the rare privilege of having, what I would like to qualify as 'unique', conversations with my Spiritual Guru Swami Bodhananda on nine chosen themes. These conversations, apart from being a window for me to see the mind of the Seer, were opportunities to know myself better and redefine my experiences according to a new set of ideas, attitudes and responses.

This volume is a collection of the nine conversations which took place between me and Pujya Swamiji, in New Delhi last summer. It is in the form of my questions and comments, and Swamiji's responses and counterpoints. The nine themes which we selected to dialogue on, ranged from outlines of

Vedanta to what essentially constitutes the quest for knowledge. The listing of the themes of conversations in this book does not follow the order in which they took place.

It was very interesting to listen to Swamiji's viewpoints since I was anticipating clichéd 'spiritual' answers from him on issues of volatile sociocultural dilemmas and the stark realities of life such as pain and death. Often Swamiji surprised me with very specific responses to issues which I thought are difficult to comment upon such as death, body, the future of 'consciousness studies' in the context of brain research and other reductionistic paradigms. One such response of Swamiji helped me to rethink about the conceptualisations we make to understand body and physical functions. I shared with him my worry that the urge to express in and through the body is so strong that I cannot imagine what I will do when my body will no more be available for me one fine morning. His response was: "To me, body is a series of information, and is a modification of eternal consciousness which is my real identity. Hence the end of one body is not the end of me or my expressions. The body need not be gross and heavy with physical extensions. It can be very subtle and still be expressing my intentions and energies. I do agree with you that there should be a mechanism for self-expression. Just as the computer chips are becoming smaller and smaller while containing more and more information, the body can be subtler and smaller."

I immensely enjoyed having these nine self-transforming conversations with Swami Bodhananda. They reflect many questions to which most of us seek answers. These dialogues are intended for daily meditations, repeated readings and discussions, reference and study. I wish you good reading.

My sincere thanks are due to Pujya Swami Bodhananda who agreed to talk with me and fully participated in our discussions in spite of his busy schedule. I thank my friends and all those with whom I discussed about these conversations and who encouraged the publication of this book. I also thank my publishers, Srishti Publishers, who have brought out the book in this beautiful manner.

Sangeetha Menon

27th March, 2002

1

Scientific and Spiritual Quest

■ The urge 'to know' is a distinctive characteristic of the human mind. What are we really trying to know? Is there anything common in scientific and spiritual quests?

We try to know about that which is invariable in our experiences, which is called 'truth'. It is very difficult to say in scientific terms what exactly we want to know. If we already know what we want to know, then there is no need of enquiry. It is a 'cat and mouse play' between epistemology and ontology.

I must admit that we are motivated by the urge to know. But we do not know what we want to know until we reach there, which may never happen. So it is a quest, and a question which is never ending and which has no complete answer. It seems that in the ultimate knowledge there will be nothing to know. In spirituality, we call it a state of being. In science, they talk about 'uncertainty principle'. And philosophy talks about the 'openness of mind'. Still, I feel there will be continuous refinement of knowledge and needs leading to deeper understanding of the structure of reality. The purpose of the control that we exercise over nature, outside and inside, will also be refined resulting in enhanced quality and durability of human life.

We try to know about that which is invariable in our experiences, which is called 'truth'.

Our mind is so structured that it is motivated by the urge to know. Knowledge has to correspond to the object of knowledge. That involves a certain *a priori* sense of the ontological nature of the object unless the object is available for verification and experimentation. Thus you have material sciences that deal with objects of senses, ethical and aesthetic sciences that deal with the nature of goodness and beauty, and spiritual sciences dealing with ultimate nature and the wholeness of reality.

■ Science is based on the experimental method. Spiritual quest is based on ideas, imagination and contemplation. Can the two enrich each other?

I do not believe in that kind of classification. Science uses imagination and contemplation. Spirituality involves experimentation, questioning and doubt. That is why a spiritual man is not a mad man or an incompetent person. Spirituality deals with the wholeness of things whereas science deals with specialised and observable areas of life and experiences.

Spirituality tries to integrate the available knowledge into the mystery of life whereas science is interested or capable of dealing only with that aspect of life which comes under its observation and the parameters of instruments. Spirituality is more comprehensive than science. It deals with life in totality more than science. It involves subtle values which science is not capable of dealing with. For example, the whole world of meaning that is constituted of happiness, purpose, and future of mankind is alien to the language of science.

■ Human cloning gives the possibility for the preservation of identity. Will the philosophical notion of 'subjectivity' be affected by the scientific advance towards physical preservation?

In the first place a clone cannot be the exact replica of the original. A clone grows up in a different environment and is denied the exact historical and environmental background of the original. And I do not think that the same environment can be recreated for the growing up clone. Creation of two identical clones is not possible at the present level of scientific progress. Subjectivity is so unique that it cannot be replicated. You may create similar clones. They cannot be identical. Therefore subjectivity can never be threatened by cloning. Cloning could create confusions in social relationships just as in the case of two people who have got similar facial features could impersonate each other and create confusions in the minds of people. Though you can impersonate another's voice or gestures, on deeper enquiry it will be easy to distinguish the pretender from the original.

■ Could moral issues bridge science and the spiritual?

I see no conflict between science and spirituality. A spiritual person is grounded in the world of facts and material relationships. In the first place I dismiss the idea that spirituality is opposed to the material world. Since there is no conflict between spirituality and material world you do not need a bridge. Laws of physical science govern man's relationship with the material world. His relationship with another being is governed by moral science. His concern for ultimate values and his own self is governed by spiritual science. Actually man is a function of all these aspects of existence.

I see no conflict between science and spirituality.

■ A person trained in science could be exemplary in understanding the principles underlying the material forces of nature. But he need not be capable enough of understanding the complexities of his own mind, relationships, families etc. A good scientist need not be a good philosopher. A good philosopher could be quite ignorant about the scientific laws and principles by which nature works.

I do not agree with your proposition. A good scientist must be a good philosopher. And a good philosopher must have a grasp of the scientific worldview. Einstein was a good philosopher. Kant had a great understanding of science. Those you are talking about are philosophers and academicians who merely deal with words and scientists who are trained in one branch of science and lack an overall worldview! Both fall into the category of scholars you mentioned.

A spiritual person has an intuitive understanding if not a technical understanding of the working of the world, of the human mind and its motives and purposes, and of the wholeness of existence. A spiritual person may not be able to design a spaceship or understand the intricacies of quantum physics. And a scientist may not be able to stop his heartbeat and sit for long hours in meditation. But these are all technical details. What is important is the 'spirit', or the 'science' of the whole phenomena.

- Physical sciences can be included under more specific and definite enterprises since they have a firm mathematical foundation. But philosophy is more a contemplative discipline, and can be regarded as part of sociocultural events at different historical times.

Science cannot be free from historical contexts. Philosophy cannot be free from scientific advancements. What you contemplate is the data in front of you, both subjective and objective, trying to get insights into those realms that are beyond your present state of knowledge.

- As cultural societies and communities we have various and different belief systems, imaginations, ideas etc. A global consensus can be generated and technology built only through science. Science is a major uniting force. Philosophy cannot create such consensus in terms of understanding nature and its forces, nor comforts or advancements in technology.

In one way I agree with you that science and technology are trans-cultural and are global unifiers whereas philosophy is locked into cultural and regional contexts. But let me remind you, when a philosophical system arises, it arises as a unifying force: unifying cultures, material knowledge and human spiritual aspirations. Philosophy and science are two legs of humanity. When science takes one step forward, philosophy appears to be left behind. But the next step is taken by philosophy. Then science in turn appears to have been left behind. But both contribute towards the march of humankind. For example, Marxism was a philosophy based on science trying to unite humanity all over the world. Democracy and open markets are political and economic ideals that appeal to humanity all over the world. So too, evangelical religions and even colonialism were similar attempts, however inadequate, to unite humanity. These were all bold attempts on the part of humankind to create global consciousness.

■ Science is founded on universal laws that are further validated by mathematics. Does philosophy follow uniform global laws as guiding principles to create and perceive uniformity amidst diverse phenomena?

Initially philosophy followed logical formulations that were based on words and their defined meanings. And now we find it to be a limited medium to understand truth and to formulate universal laws. But there are certain universal laws that philosophy and religion have propounded that have stood the test of time. For example, 'all men are mortal', 'love unites and hate divides', 'we are children of the same father', 'world is one family', 'truth alone triumphs' are some of those formulations which are accepted as unimpeachable universal laws, as powerful as the law of gravity. And, nowadays philosophy borrows heavily from the world of mathematics and science in its enquiry into reality. I find increasing convergence between science, philosophy and spirituality.

■ 'Love unites and hate divides'. This is more an abstract formulation than a law. Because, for the same end result of love I can kill a person or dedicate all my life to him/her. That means the goal, which is love, could be materialised through violent as well non-violent means. So, how can the law still be universal in respective of different means and motives serving the same goal?

A law has reference to a framework. Newton's law may not be applicable in the Einsteinian world. That does not mean Newton's law has no applicability. A lover and his/her beloved are united in the energy of love. Outside their field they may harbour hatred. Or in time one may hate the other when he/she has no more love for her/him. That does not mean that the law that love unites is faulty. The true meaning of love is love for all. When true love arises it has to unite all. I do not think that the law that love unites is just a wish or a simple moral principle. It is a law that governs facts.

The true meaning of love is love for all.

■ Love can be a strong dividing force too. For example, the love for the country and land can cause civil wars, like those happening in Chechnya or Israel, or even within a family. Extreme love for a particular family member can create hatred for others.

Again, you are confusing between frameworks. Love for the country unites people belonging to different tribes and races. Patriotism is a highly unifying force. At the same time when two countries are pitted against each other, between those two countries, patriotism creates conflict. That is not the fault of love. It is our inability to extend love to those who do not belong to our country. Therefore what is necessary is to expand your love to all the peoples of the world. This may require communication, transportation, movement of people, interlinking facilities, open markets etc.

- Science is founded on universal laws. At the same time science is ready to change, improve and perceive truth as different, since it abides by the Popperian 'falsifiability theory'. But spirituality and philosophy seem to be a finished product without a chance for improvising. They begin and end with absolute *a priori* principles and truths that cannot be questioned.

Spirituality, religion and even philosophy deal with the ultimate objectives of life. These objectives are subjected to questioning, reflection and modification, which have been happening throughout human history. Ideas of God, hell and heaven are changing. The meaning of ultimate happiness or felicity itself is changing. I do not see philosophy and religion as closed books. Just as scientists find it difficult to break out of old paradigms and continue to cling on to outdated ideas, so too in spirituality and religion people with entrenched interests find difficulty in breaking new ground.

The meaning of ultimate happiness or felicity itself is changing.

Even the most orthodox religious institution like the Roman Catholic Church is constantly evolving and updating their understanding of God, Christ's relationship with God, his mission in this world, the meaning of sin, fall from grace and final deliverance.

I do not agree with your idea that spirituality and philosophy are frozen into inflexible positions.

■ Let me bring to your attention the specific case of *mahāvākyās, Upāniṣādic* statements. They are *a priori* and absolute principles that have to be realised. The process of realisation begins with the presentation of these statements through scriptures and ends with their personal realisation. What is that which is changing and evolving in between the beginning and the end event in this case, namely the presentation of these statements by the Guru and the final realisation by the student?

Tattvamasi is the encapsulation of one of the greatest spiritual insights. We are not sure whether this statement actually and fully captures the spirit of that insight. A person who could inspire others by facilitating a new worldview uttered this statement. If you see the history of that statement you find different masters interpreting the statement differently, sometime contradictorily, but still clinging on to it. This adherence was because of the potentiality of the statement to invoke a variety of inspiring moods and experiences, whose contours might have varied but the content of which remained the same. I think that *Tattvamasi* represents a universal principle or law that expresses the relationship between the experiencing individual and his ultimate destiny. It may also expound a relationship between the beginning and end of a phenomenon or the nature of opposing and contradictory energies or the final unity of all manifestations.

Since *Tattvamasi* deals with a dynamically living and evolving universe it also has to be understood dynamically. Its applicability is universal and it has its implication in every field of human activity. I, as a devotee of that statement, feel that it states the ultimate law of existence.

■ Science can unify humans transcending cultures, societies and institutions through scientific laws and understanding of nature. But how can spiritual movements unify humankind transcending their sociocultural differences?

I do not think that either science or spirituality can easily unify humankind. I think something else works in the case of unity. Humankind is actually a unified phenomenon. Men are related to nature and to one another but at the same time there are disuniting factors also. We find a tension between unifying and individualistic forces in actual human history. There will be no time when we can end this tension.

I do not think that either science - or spirituality can easily unify humankind.

If the 'ideal unification' that you mention, is political or economic unification, it might or might not happen. Individuals pursuing their personal agenda will continue to create conflicts and convergences. History is a record of convergence and divergence of individual's interest with collective interest. When we talk about 'unification' it means that knowledge is available freely, anybody can buy property anywhere in the world, anybody can contend for power and position for any office in the world, anybody can choose to live anywhere in the world, anybody can choose to practice any religion, etc.

Apart from these we do not understand the meaning of unity. Unity is an evolving concept. Also, unity exists in nature. I think we deal with phantoms of words. What is required is true and dispassionate analysis of these words and relating them to actual situations.

■ Which do you think, science or philosophy, could give a better understanding of reality?

Together, philosophy and science give an approximate understanding of reality. Science influences philosophy. Philosophy influences science. After all both are structures of human thinking and ways of encountering human experiences and creating meaning and knowledge out of them. Scientific discoveries have philosophical implications. And, philosophical questions need scientific answers. The tendency to divide spirituality, philosophy and science will slowly disappear, as areas of concerns converge and new linguistic and mathematical models of questioning arise where both spiritual and material questions will have implications for human survival.

■ What is your view on the many attempts to see similar ideas in science and philosophy, especially through quantum mechanical research?

Quantum mechanics takes scientists to a realm where old worldviews and theoretical assumptions collapse. The scientist is compelled to use language and metaphors, which are similar to those, used by spiritualists and philosophers. I am not sure whether they describe the same phenomena or whether they deal with the same reality. I feel that scientists are clearer about their fields than philosophers and spiritualists are about their fields of study. However, all of them face the problem of 'clouds of unknowing'.

Scientists are clearer about their fields than philosophers and spiritualists are about their fields of study.

Scientists are able to split atoms and generate energy using their knowledge of nuclear physics. I do not see the same clarity among the philosophers and so-called spiritualists. I do not think that the hasty conclusions regarding the convergence of matter and mind in Quantum Mechanics made by Capra and Zukov have been profound. But I would encourage such thought processes. After all reality is one.

- What is your view on the recent recommendation by India's University Grants Commission for including Astrology in the science departments of universities?

I do not think astrology is a science. Nor should human energy be wasted in astrological formulations.

However, humankind loves to devise quick-fix methods to divine the future. Astrology will have an entertainment or gratification value just as cigarettes, liquor, cinema etc. have. They all satisfy certain human needs. We need such mind-managing techniques also to deal with uncertainties, though they may not be productive and contributive to human health and growth.

Therefore, if there is a market value for astrological predictions and if they satisfy the human need to overcome anxiety and tension, I do not find any reason why there should not be institutes to train astrologers. Let the end-user decide what he needs. If it is extremely harmful to human health, both psychological and social, it is the duty of the government to initiate a debate and decide whether astrology should form a subject in academic studies. Left to myself I would outrightly reject astrology as a course in the science departments of Indian universities.

At the same time I do not find any harm in offering it as a separate course and sending astrology graduates all over the world to earn precious foreign exchange for India. When people come to know that all the predictions made are not correct (according to the law of probability some predictions can turn out to be correct), the same consumer will refuse to buy the product. Then nobody will clamour for a degree in astrology. Perhaps, then we can give a temporary burial to astrology. But I am sure the human mind being what it is, the ghost of astrology will again rise up, stalking presumptuously and claiming respectability.

■ Indian philosophy deals basically with the spiritual self. At the same time it also deals with the body and pleasures. For example, we have literature on medicine, sexual life, material gains etc. How can the physical and the spiritual quest go together?

Indian philosophy does not talk about an exclusive and isolated self. It talks about self-experience inherent in all material and mental events. It also talks about a self that can nourish the material and mental life. As a spiritual discipline, Indian philosophy deals with your food, your environment, your psyche and your body. Spirit is the wholeness of energies.

Spirit is the wholeness of energies.

It is not an isolated entity opposed or distinct from something else. That is why in India all enterprises are geared towards spiritual realisation whether it is having food, applying medicine, building a house, singing songs or debating philosophy. Anything you do is geared towards spiritual realisation. There is no conflict between matter, mind and spirit.

- Science talks about the physical universe. Philosophy also talks about the physical. Why then is philosophy given a spiritual component and not science?

Science is more materialistic, physical and reductionistic, whereas philosophy includes mind, values, and purpose, and is more holistic. Philosophy involves an element of change and transformation whereas science deals with cold facts. Therefore, philosophy gives direction to science, whereas science gives energy to philosophy. Perhaps that is why philosophy is nearer to spirituality than science. But a situation has come when the distinction between philosophy and science is narrowing down, and surely the distinction between science, philosophy and spirituality will also narrow down.

- Increasingly science is realising that reality is constituted of quantum mechanical states, which no more 'obeys' the classical rule of linearity and causality. The physical universe which we perceive is only apparent and is almost non-existent. But with our ordinary eyes we are unable to see the fluctuating quantum states of the physical universe and are able to respond only to a three-dimensional sense of reality when the actual reality could be multidimensional. Perhaps, spirituality or *Yoga* can give us a 'third eye' to view the physical world in its original quantum state, and may be the realised *Yogis* are able to perceive the physical universe in its quantum state.

We are confusing here between realms and frameworks of existence. Understanding of reality depends upon the instrument through which you look and how it impacts on the observer's consciousness and how much the observer can manipulate reality with the help of instruments for desired goals and objectives. If you say that the physical world has no reality and only the quantum world has reality, then that would be a hasty statement. All of them have realities in their own realms.

A *Yogi* talks about a reality conditioned by his disciplines, his prior understanding of reality and his way of interpreting experience. It is absurd to think that with the present knowledge of *Yoga* and mind and *Yogic* disciplines one could have an understanding of the quantum world that the scientists talk about. That understanding requires scientific training. Because that is how scientists have constructed their instruments and interpreted their experiences. I do not feel that the scientist's and the *Yogi's* methodologies will converge as they exist today. The *Yogi* has no way of knowing the quantum reality by simply practicing *Yogāsanās* and meditation techniques without a rigorous scientific discipline. But scientists can learn valuable lessons of mind control and the *Yogi*'s worldview and ways of interpreting experiences in understanding their scientific mind and re-defining their ways of looking at or interpreting reality. There is no sudden enlightenment by which the entire complex quantum world is revealed in one go. That would make the whole process silly and it reveals a mindset that takes reality to be homogeneous and simple. Reality is heterogeneous and complex.

■ If reality is heterogeneous and complex what is that which we are seeking in the name of unity? What is the unifying factor which runs through the variety?

Heterogeneity and complexity are not against unity. It only means that unity is very rich and dynamic, and incorporates variety and unpredictability. When you ask for a 'unifying factor' you are asking for something extraneous which will land you in the fallacy of *regress ad infinitum*. You have to find a unifying factor within the complexity. Otherwise we will be like the tribal who searches for the 'tick' of the clock outside the clock. Again, the tendency to see the unifying factor outside the variety reflects the same mindset that looks for a spiritual factor other than and opposed to the material and mental. In the process you neither understand the mental, the material or the spiritual.

Heterogeneity and complexity are not against unity.

- Ultimately science seeks the oneness of the multitude. How does one realise the oneness, according to you?

When you talk about 'oneness' do you mean the oneness as the integral nature of the multitudinous and variegated universe, or are you talking about the one single entity from which the multitudinous universe arises? I think these types of questions have to be probed not exclusively but in an integrated manner. That requires a totally different approach. Instead of looking for something extraneous and deductive just look with an open mind. Even if you look for something it will only be an open-ended look.

- There is one science, but many philosophies. How can one find the right or true philosophy?

There are many sciences too: many propositions, many ways of doing research, many provisional answers. Similarly there are many philosophies offering provisional answers. But the stem of science is thick and clear like a palm tree whereas the philosophical forest is made up of bamboo reeds and grasses. You do not find any thick stem anywhere in the philosophical forest. Every philosopher stands isolated and unto himself. But that is the very nature of philosophy. It deals with mind and ideas whereas science deals with observable, measurable and quantifiable material phenomena.

- Medieval and modern European philosophy gave rise to modern science. Why did Indian thought fail to inspire and sustain scientific quest?

I will respond to this question in two streams. First, modern science in its present rigour and intensity appeared in the cold regions where people asked practical questions of survival. They had to find practical answers for their questions that dominated their daily existence. Second, a large number of Europeans, maybe 50 per cent in England, went outside Europe taking great risks, and the variety of experiences challenged their mind to ask rational and unconventional questions. All of them geared to their survival-needs in hostile and alien lands. It is these two factors that contributed to the growth of science and technology and the emergence of a civil society in the Western world. The enlightened man of the West came to think that he could shape his destiny by asking questions, processing data in his mind, constructing working models and applying them in his physical environment. That would have been a great moment in history when man realised that he could control the environment rather than remaining a hapless creature. India or China did not have these advantages caused by extremes in environment and climate, and large numbers of people migrating and exposing themselves to different lands and climates. Also, there was less need to control nature since nature was very friendly to them.

- What are the distinct and common goals of science and philosophy according to you in the future?

Survival of humanity and life on earth, and if it exists anywhere else there also, is the goal of all enterprises, scientific or philosophical. Because, I find that survival of the self-aware individual is the fundamental purpose of any pursuit. There are no other purposes. The purposes of science and philosophy converge in the promotion and nourishment of self-aware subjective consciousness, which is humanity.

2

Spirituality and Human Mind

■ What is 'to be spiritual' and what is 'spirituality'?

Spirit is the invisible ground of all visible manifestations, of the world of mind and matter. We deduce the existence of the spirit from the ever-changing nature of the world. Change cannot exist without a changeless substratum. Spirit is realised through the detached mind of the experiencer. The spirit can be invoked as health, energy and intelligence for enriching human life. Spirit is the raw material for the creation of the stellar constellations, the rain forests and the brain of a baby. Spirit is infinite information packed in dimensionless space which is the cause for all transformations.

Spirit is health, energy, and intelligence.

■ From your answer what I understand is that the spirit is nothing more than a utility to conceive of an abstract concept in order to integrate the diversity and multiplicity of experiences. Do you agree?

As we go into the depth of subtlety I find no difference between reality and concepts. Therefore by calling 'spirituality' an abstract concept you are only giving it a new point of view. A new point of view does not change the actual picture.

■ If it does not matter whether 'spirituality' is called an abstract concept or otherwise, what does it matter if an experience is termed a 'spiritual experience'? What is the significance of being or experiencing something as 'spiritual'?

Spiritual life is a deepened experience of all-encompassing existence. It enriches the individual's life and awakens him/her to his/her cosmic potentialities and make him/her realise that he/she is a point at which the entire existence finds self-expression.

■ Perhaps, we will come back to this issue a little later. Is 'spirituality' antagonistic to being 'materialistic'?

That depends up on your understanding of materialism. If you say that matter is divorced of intelligence, consciousness, and is something available for manipulation by individual desire and greed, then I think spirituality is deeper and higher than materialism.

If you consider matter as an expression of spirit, I would see no conflict or dichotomy between material aspirations and spiritual experiences.

■ The attempt to understand or explain spirit in terms of matter and matter in terms of spirit cannot be tantamount to giving specific definitions for them.

Could you please explain what makes something or the same thing/event/experience material or spiritual, if you think that the classification of 'material' or 'spiritual' is a matter of perspective?

Invisible matter is spirit. Visible spirit is matter. The point at which the divergence takes place is human consciousness. Spirit can be realised as the deep subjectivity of the self-conscious individual.

■ If the spirit is the deep subjectivity of the individual what is his body?

Body, which is subject to change and which is available for objective experience, is a visible expression or a formulation of spirit.

■ This is an understanding of the body in terms of the spirit that can be approached only through non-verbal understanding. Could you please say what is body in more concrete terms and why you think it does not fall into the 'subjectivity' of the individual, since earlier you defined spirit as the 'deep subjectivity of the individual'?

Body is an object of experience and hence cannot be included in the definition of the subject. But body can be included in the proximity of the subject. The structure of the body has a certain correlation with the history of the individual and his spiritual identity. So, I would consider that body-mind-spirit constitute the totality of individuality at any given moment.

Body-mind-spirit constitute the totality of individuality at any given moment.

- Is 'being spiritual' or 'spirituality' a global trans-cultural phenomenon?

Human existence has a global as well as local content. Even global experiences cannot be understood except through local instrumentality. Therefore, I do not see any purpose in dividing spirituality into local and global. It is unholistic, and it will not reveal the complexity of the phenomenon.

- What is it that which makes an otherwise ordinary experience 'spiritual'?

Just to paraphrase poet Shelly, 'he is wise who can see the whole ocean in a drop of water, the stellar constellation in a grain of sand, and the face of god in the smile of a baby'. There is no spiritual experience that is divorced of the momentary experiences, just as there is no water that is divorced of two atoms of hydrogen and one atom of oxygen.

- I think I am still unclear about the single component that would make the revolutionary change for an ordinary experience to its being/becoming spiritual!

An ordinary experience of a healthy man becomes spiritual when he sees the invariable self in the changing phenomena of experiences.

- I said earlier that spirituality is an abstract concept for the holistic understanding of diversity and multiplicity. What is the connection between being spiritual, and values, duties and responsibilities, since these four are correlated in most cultures?

Any phenomenon has a vertical dimension and a horizontal dimension, if I may express it in the geometric paradigm. Vertically a phenomenon has gross, then a subtle, then a causal and then a transcendental dimension. Horizontally they have corresponding relatedness to the totality of phenomena. And thus spiritual understanding involves values and duties that help the individual to exist integrally related to all these dimensions. Values and duties are the natural expressions of an integrated mind.

■ I would like to ask a question related to the earlier one and about the popular notions of having transcendental experiences. Spirituality is often identified with having mystic or extraordinary or transcendental experiences. Abiding by certain values and being obliged to perform duties seem to relate the individual to the ordinary world of duality, and not transcendence. Where does the transcendence of spirituality emerge in relationships and sociocultural exchanges?

The transcendental is not unrelated to the terrestrial or the ordinary, just as the root system of the tree is not divorced from the flowers and foliage of the tree. Therefore true spirituality is seeing the whole in an insignificant event rather than condemning the event to the realm of the mundane and then trying to work towards imaginary sensations.

True spirituality is seeing the whole in an insignificant event.

I do not deny the poetic beauty of such imaginary experiences. But they themselves are not whole and complete, and often border on an imbalance of mind. Such experiences are not holistic but are divisive and exclusive which may give them a sense of importance and historical value. This does not make the individual a spiritual person. Such an individual can only be likened to a genetically modified mouse showing extraordinary behaviour.

■ I am very happy to hear that you consider experiences which are merely classified as 'spiritual' to be parochial and not real. But then why do you think mankind has always given an 'extraordinariness' or an 'etherealness' to certain experiences which were labelled as nothing but 'spiritual' or 'mystic'?

I cannot help it if meanings of words change over a period of time. Nor am I opposed to extraordinary happenings in the field of mind and thought. When humanity comes to a point of stagnation, entrepreneurial people think non-conventionally and that creates powerful, emotional and intellectual energies that give a new direction to society. I would consider that such experiences belong to the realms of politics and history, or at best to the cultural and sociological fields.

Spirituality is deeper than history though it includes historical processes. It is not a cumulative process. Every moment of the spirit is complete and full. That is the meaning of '*pūrṇamada pūrṇamidaṃ*', 'the cause is whole, the effect also is whole'. Unfortunately history takes note only of the historical content of the spiritual people and not the spiritual content of the historical people.

- In line with the discussion we are having, let me submit a simple question: What is an experience? What makes it ordinary or transcendental? What is the set of rules or guidelines that has the non-historical authority to make such a classification?

An experience is that which is presented to the experiencer's consciousness. I do not believe in such classification of experiences into transcendental and ordinary. All experiences are extraordinary. All experiences have the power and authority of the conscious experiencer. The classification of experiences into 'transcendental' and 'ordinary' is the need of the ordinary individual, because of his insecurity, and for authoritarian purposes. The only authority for an experience is the experiencer's consciousness. No experience, transcendental or mundane, can be greater than the consciousness of the experiencer.

- If so, do you think that a paradigm shift has taken place in the realm of human experiences where the human would consider experiences as qualitatively different if not ordinary or extraordinary? Can the diversity and the multiplicity in the kind of experiences humankind has had, or is having, all be traced to psychoanalytic, reductive notions of insecurity and authoritativeness?

I did not mean to say that all experiences could be reduced to psychoanalytic concepts. I talked about various dimensions of experiences: vertical, horizontal and collective. I also said that their permutations and combinations offer a rich variety of experiences and evolutionary and devolutionary possibilities.

Divisions like ordinary and extraordinary are both within the realm of mind and matter.

When I said that divisions like ordinary and extraordinary are both within the realm of mind and matter, I only meant that a person of holistic vision does not classify experiences that way. But a man of parochial vision with his limited intellect will try to understand experiences through classifications and comparisons.

■ What is the relationship between spirituality, religion and theology? Where do spirituality, religion and theology meet or part?

In 'religion' I will include the historical experiences of human races. Theology is an intellectual adaptation of those historical epoch making experiences. I will include religion in the causal dimension with a glimpse of the transcendent or the spirit. To me 'spirituality' is more comprehensive. I will say that Buddha's 'compassion', Christ's 'non-violence', Kṛṣṇa's 'unconditional love', Socrates' 'relentless questioning' and the *Upaniṣads'* via negativa '*neti neti*' are expressions of spiritual insights.

■ Both religion and mysticism have their history going back to primitive humans and cultures. It would seem that certain experiences which we might today call 'tribal' or 'primitive' have led or lead to the development of belief systems, to the forming of organised institutions of religion and forming philosophies about them. Can spirituality be separated or understood without looking into the 'tribal' and 'primitive' cultures or experiences one could have or has had?

Spirituality has to stand the test of rationalism, and the historical and collective experiences of races. Therefore, an expanding mind, which I consider the sign of spirituality, will not be averse to any human experience. In fact a holistic mind invites all experiences and integrates them, and invokes new experiences. It is a very dynamic and fluid state.

■ Is spiritual experience a religious experience? Recent experiments have shown that religious experiences can be traced to neural firings in specific areas of the brain. Are religious experiences open-ended and evolving or brain-generated, independent of the history of the individual? These experiments have also shown that from an historical account it is mostly people who suffered from severe epileptic seizures who had more and periodic visions!

I am not a votary of exclusive experiences as candidates for spirituality.

Since I am not a votary of exclusive experiences as candidates for spirituality I do not think that epileptic seizures or *yogic* trances or personal crises are necessary for spiritual experiences. But I do believe that there is a correlation between brain, mind and spirituality. Evolution of the brain and the content of the mind, and the expression of potentialities of spirit are all related phenomena.

As a holistic person I believe, in and experience no division between spirit, mind and brain. Brain-mind facilities, and their evolutionary characteristics, are important structures for the manifestation of spirit. You can call it the intelligent spirit!

- Do you think therefore that these new approaches or studies which are brain centred, and which find the veracity of spiritual experiences or religious experiences based on neural correlations will not undermine their uniqueness and distort their depth?

These approaches will not undermine the uniqueness of spiritual experiences but will undermine their claim for depth. I think these experiments should go on to sift the grain from the chaff though they may create their own chaff in the process.

- Are spiritual experiences open ended and prone to biological evolution?

Spiritual experiences are not unique specific experiences. Spiritual experience inheres in all experiences. Therefore in spite of all changes and complexities in human experiences, the quality of spiritual experience will remain the same, which is expressed by statements like 'truth and love are universal and a-historical'.

- Can spirituality and complexity of mind be compared and, further, can both be standards for measuring intelligence?

If your question is whether spirituality is contingent upon the complexity of human brain/mind, my answer is 'no'. If your question is whether the complexity of brain and mind will contribute to the expressiveness and variety of human experiences my answer is 'yes'. I would not like to put the 'horse behind the cart', meaning, making holistic experience contingent upon the complexity of brain. But I would maintain that holistic experience would contribute to the progressive evolution and complexity of brain.

- Could it be that the complex is spiritual, and the spiritual is intelligent? The more complex a system, the more spiritual it is, and the more intelligent it is!

I would put it in a different way. The more spiritual you are, the more you are able to integrate complexities and the more you are able to manifest intelligence. Meaning, an intelligent person is better able to function holistically both in complex and simple situations. And, the ultimate value of his experiences, whether the situation is complex or simple, will be the same. The motor force of increasing complexities is not the blind interaction but the intelligent coordination of energies.

- A complex system is defined as that which performs nonlinear functions, and that which need not follow rules and always show expected responses. Consciousness, for example, is considered to be a complex phenomenon. Do you think research in consciousness studies, which is now becoming an interdisciplinary enterprise of philosophers, neurobiologists, linguists and so on, will have direct links with our understanding or even creation of spiritual experiences?

Intelligence also is defined as 'complexity'. I am happy that modern scientific research tends to include the datum of consciousness in its experimental pursuits, which will make the scientist's mind more holistic and make him/her think and have more extraordinary ways of looking at reality and fashion tools to conduct research.

Neurobiological studies, experiments and research in the field of artificial intelligence, man-machine interfaces, internet revolution, the genome project etc. will help scientists reach new levels of experiences. But I will not consider them as spiritual. To be spiritual is to integrate all levels of experiences, individualistic and collective, transcendental and mundane, at the border-line of the individual and the cosmic in the consciousness of the subject.

To be spiritual is to integrate all levels of experiences.

- If we can create a very holistically responding machine based on artificial intelligence, how would do you think that the phenomenon of spirituality would be addressed?

That depends upon our understanding and control of what is history. When we are able to move back into time and exactly re-create the Aurangazebs and Socrateses in their historical habitats and move into the future and create their future histories, or in a situation where man, machine and nature freely exchange their intelligence, perhaps, that may be possible.

After all man is a machine made by history and biology. And in this context I would not even discount the possibility of interstellar intelligence interspersing with human intelligence and creating new vistas in cognitive processes.

- It looks as though human life, or for that matter biological life, has a purpose which is more acceptable and noble than the purpose of a machine. What do you think makes the purpose of human life more unique? What is the purpose of human life?

What make a human life unique are the individual's subjectivity and his ability to judge an experience and create values. A machine does not possess that ability. Hence human life is considered nobler than the machine's life. In that sense the individual subject is the measure of values and is able to penetrate into the world of truth, beauty and goodness. The purpose of human life is nothing other than what the human envisages and creates for himself/herself. But objectively I can say that the purpose of human life is to expand and encompass.

- What do you think is the contribution of Indian systems of thought and philosophies to spiritual experiences or 'to be spiritual'?

Several systems have appeared and disappeared in the world and some of their contributions are still alive in the racial consciousness of humankind. Contributions of some others have gone deep into the unconscious. I do not think that human history began 6000 or 7000 years ago. I see that all races and people belonging to all nations have contributed to the evolution of human consciousness. It is difficult to compare and assess the value and volume of their contributions. But from known history we can say that the Greeks, Romans, Egyptians, Jews, Chinese, Incas, Mayans and Hindus have contributed in a big way to the evolution of human civilisation.

I am sceptical about India's contribution to the evolution of the present scientific, technological and industrial civilisation, except in terms of being a source of raw material and a market for finished products during the industrial revolution. But the time is slowly emerging where some of the survival skills, both mental and physical that Indians have evolved over a period of time under chaotic and starvation conditions, may contribute in a considerable way to the survival of modern humans who are facing unimaginable chaos, alienation, violence, social disruption, inequality and poverty conditions.

- There is consensus about the contribution of Indian mathematics and Ayurvedic system of medicine. It is also debated that much of what is today accepted as modern science was the result of the Muslim invasion of India which led to the translation of valuable Sanskrit texts to Arabic which were later translated into Latin by the Europeans!

India as well as the Muslim world is far behind the Western countries. They are still not able to catch up with the West in the field of science, technology, in offering a comfortable standard of living to their people and in evolving a participatory system of decision-making in the creation and distribution of wealth. The health of the root system of a tree is known by the health of its branches. Had India been a rich country in terms of science and technology before the Muslim conquest, the first question is how did India succumb to the primitive Muslims. The second question is, why could not the Muslims, themselves, after learning so much from India, develop science and technology? Thirdly, before the development of Western science, almost all countries of the world were technologically and scientifically at the same level. Nobody could have learned much from anybody.

No doubt India and China, Greece and Rome, Egypt and Mesopotamia were superior civilisations. But what the Europeans experienced after the Middle Ages was a great paradigm shift and break from the usual way of interpreting human experiences. I do not see the point in harping on India's contribution to the scientific and technological developments of the West unless it is just to create national pride and give self-respect to Indians. The goal of India should be to lead the world in science and technology by making original contributions based on global knowledge available today. There is no point in simply saying that our contributions are not recognised when we ourselves could not develop upon our initial advantages in those fields of thought.

■ Let me keep science aside and take philosophy. There is a recent excitement in the West in the field of 'consciousness' research. When we look at the questions asked and approaches made in the West we can see a major difference when compared to approaches in Indian theoretical traditions. Another situation is that there is a lot of use and application of Indian concepts and ideas and even metaphors in Western academia without acknowledging their Indian sources. What is your response?

I do agree that after Descartes Western thinking became more objective and experimental and utilitarian than subjective, meditative and holistic, whereas India has a rich tradition of holistic approaches to the entire gamut of life. It is reflected in *Ayurveda*, *Yoga*, *Vedānta* etc. As the leading civilisation of the world, Westerners are becoming more conscious of the schizophrenic nature of their studies, research and civilisation and they are bound to look to other civilisations for insights, lessons and leads. And in this emerging scenario the Western civilisation is going to interact with other civilisations. It is simple academic ethics to acknowledge the source of an idea in the building up of knowledge. If somebody is not doing it he will be exposed whether he is in the East or West. In the modern world of intellectual property piracy, ingratitude happens everywhere.

■ An article in a recent issue of *Time* talked about the popularity of Indian *Yoga* amongst the Western elite and celebrities. And there was uproar from the intellectual and academic communities that the discussion in that article was quite untrue to real *Yoga* and that the notion of *Yoga* explained in the article pertained only to the ideas popular in the West as '*Yoga*'. What is your response?

My first response is that *Time* did yeomen service to the further propagation of *Yoga* in the Western hemisphere. A popular magazine like *Time* is a mirror of emerging trends in society. Its main job is to reflect ideas prevalent and popular in society rather than to create ideas for society. And the popular notion of *Yoga* is about simple physical exercises that can help the practitioner to connect the body to the mind and experience peace and well-being.

Academicians and practitioners may discuss deeper aspects of *Yoga* like spiritual awakening and enlightenment. *Time* has done its job by publishing a main article. Let others who are seriously devoted to *Yoga* by their personal practice propagate the true spirit of *Yoga*.

■ Do you mean to say that an accepted magazine like *Time* which creates identities and ideas need not discuss the whole and true meanings of *Yoga*, but discuss only the popular notions about it?

It is very difficult to determine the true *meaning* of an esoteric subject like *Yoga*. When you take the commentaries on the *Yogasutrās* of Patanjali you find that there are as many versions as there are commentators. Do the *Yogasutrās* accept the dualistic nature of reality? Does Patanjali teach concentration on the object or the subject? What is the relation between the subjective and the objective world? What is the practical meaning of various *siddhis* described in the *Yogasutrās*? What is understood by control of thought processes? I find that there is no agreement on any of those topics among the interpreters of *Yoga*. Therefore it would have been foolish on the part of *Time* magazine to dwell on the esoteric meaning of *Yoga* rather than on the popular perception and practice.

■ You are a Swami. Your views, if I am permitted to say so, sound radical and revolutionary. How do you define your identity and what is your role as a saint from India?

I do not know whether my views are radical and different from those of other saints and swamis. However, all my views are developed from my understanding of *Advaita Vedānta*, a strong feeling of love for and pride in my motherland, and from my eagerness to participate in the creation of a dynamic global community. In the process I myself want to grow and unfold my full spiritual, emotional and intellectual potential. I think this much would help you define my identity, which task I leave to you.

■ Will the increasing number of spiritual movements and institutions in the West and the East influence global societies and communities for their overall sustainability?

Increase in religious activity is a mixed blessing just as any human activity is.

Recently there was a global spiritual leaders' meet in the UN. This was organised parallel to the NGO global meet that was also organised by the UN. After the collapse of the communist regimes of the erstwhile Soviet Union and other East European countries, they have been experiencing a resurgence of religious and spiritual movements.

In communist China there are new spiritual movements like the *Falun Gong* that attracts large number of youngsters in their daily spiritual meetings. The proselytising religions like Christianity, Islam and Buddhism are also spreading their wings in the Americas and East Asian countries. And I think this religious and spiritual renaissance after the collapse of communism and the serious concerns that thinking people or intellectuals have against the indiscriminate industrialisation of the world are contributing towards a global awareness for addressing world issues and problems, transcending national and sectarian considerations.

At the same time religious groups are mainly responsible for the ethnic and sectarian violence that is erupting all over the world whether it is in Kashmir, Chechnya, Kosova, Philippines or Sudan, or anywhere else in the world. I think that the globalisation process is mainly the effect of industrialisation of the world. Religious awareness that is manifesting as global movements is only an aftermath of this process. Therefore, I should say that increase in religious activity is a mixed blessing just as any human activity is.

■ Religious institutions are natural offshoots of spiritual movements and philosophies. Religion also seems to be often the reason for social turmoil and ideological and ritualistic clashes. Can we do away with religion and focus only on spiritual movements, and make spirituality a-religious and a-institutional?

You cannot quarantine spirituality from the defects of human greed and need for collective identities.

As I told you earlier spirituality is entwined with religion, science, economics and technology. Hence you cannot quarantine spirituality from the defects of human greed and need for collective identities.

Perhaps, a few individuals can be spiritually

awakened and be free from the defects of greed, violence, envy and fear. It might take sufficient material advancement creating a situation of plenitude and psychological emancipation from deep-rooted fears and insecurities for the full spiritual flowering of all individuals who constitute global communities.

I think that strife, struggle and sectarian violence will continue along with the domination of one group over another, humans over the flora and fauna, the strong and knowledgeable over the weak and ignorant, males over females, elders over children, the technologically advanced over the technologically backward. Spirituality will be ineffective as a tool of social reengineering in such situations.

- Apart from the esoteric interest which spiritual thinking and philosophy can generate, can it help in bringing about better science and technology, social development and economic progress?

Spirituality enlarges our interests and concerns since it is the relentless pursuit of truth, beauty and goodness, humanity and justice. Spirituality will have its ramifications in all aspects of human endeavour. But it will be very difficult to predict the course of its unfolding.

Spirituality will have its ramifications in all aspects of human endeavour.

Spirituality is open-mindedness, integration and relentless exploration and self-expression. It is fearlessness and freedom to experiment and recreate oneself and one's environment in infinite ways. Hence spirituality is the ultimate solution for human bondage.

- India is known for its spiritual heritage. Why has not this rich heritage helped India in its social and economic progress?

Social and economic progress depends upon science, technology and the productive organisation of human and material resources. Spirituality mainly deals with the spirit and the freedom of the individual, and most often becomes hostage to the material conditions prevalent in the society.

India had a glorious past. India could build big buildings, think original thoughts in the field of mathematics, astronomy, and establish powerful empires and global trade and create world religions while the masses toiled in poverty.

But like the law of life that everything born must die, and that the dead shall be reborn again, India is also going through these phases. It had a very sad patch of history during the last 1500 years. Slowly India is emerging from the shadows and is beginning to be recognised as a worthy member of the world community of nations, learning from others and contributing to the world heritage.

3

Body, Mind and Consciousness

■ The classification of the human being into body, mind and spirit is common to classical Western and Eastern philosophies. Would you like to add any more divisions into this group for analysing the human being?

The division depends upon the understanding of the spirit, mind and body. To me the spirit is more universal, borderless and encompassing, than as some Semitic religious thinkers understand it. So too for me; mind has got a history and is cumulative, and is distinct from the brain. Mind survives the disintegration of the body and brain.

There is a certain mutuality that exists between these basic components. We can say that the spirit is the substratum for mind and body. At the same time one can say that mind and spirit are substrated on the body or brain network. It is like saying that 'space is the substratum for the pot' and 'the pot contains the space'.

There are many ambiguities and differences in the understanding of these words and resultant value systems and worldviews that philosophers uphold. But otherwise I agree with this broad division of the individual into body, mind and spirit.

■ Can you give a synoptic description of what you consider as the physical, the mental, and the spiritual?

I briefly gave a description of these terms in my previous response. Spirit, I would consider as that which is subjective, invisible, indivisible and non-sublatable, self-evident experience that cannot be objectified. In its essence, it is infinite information, and is universal and is the source of everything. Mind is the result of intentions, and intentions cause thoughts that are energies with direction and purpose. Mind tries to organise thoughts around centres that are the sources of intentions. It is the way that the spirit actualises its depths and dimensions. Mind thus has a history and is a dynamic and subtle flow that influences the ordering of the material world. There can be many minds with many dimensions and hence the classification of the mind into conscious, unconscious, subconscious, collective, individual etc. is possible. I would say that these are currents that happen in the ocean of consciousness.

Mind is the result of intentions, and intentions cause thoughts.

Intentions are eternal and uncaused. They are spontaneous. They are self-generative and almost conform to the uncertainty principle of quantum physics, whereas the body and brain are products of intentions and thoughts. They are conditions for thoughts to actualise the infinite potentialities of consciousness.

When a person dies it is the body that disintegrates along with the brain. The mind survives with his personal history. In the state of enlightenment, the mind loses its illusion of separateness and realises its potential as a channel of expressing the infinitude of the spirit.

- Since the last decade there is a revived interest in the subject of consciousness amongst neurobiologists, physicists and philosophers, all looking at the problem from new angles.

I am extremely happy that philosophers in the West (philosophers in the East had always had an interest), neurobiologists and physicists are compelled to accept consciousness as a datum in the mental and material process that creates experiences. Experience is the fundamental reality of human existence. Neurobiologists are not able to explain consciousness merely in terms of neurological and chemical processes. They see a gap between experience and such processes that can be explained only by the X factor of consciousness. So, too, quantum physicists are not able to explain the maverick behaviour of the quantum state and they posit the observer's consciousness or the innate intelligence of the observed phenomena as the cause of the unpredictable behaviour of quantum states. Philosophers find it difficult to explain processes whether it is subjective or objective without positing an abiding subject that acts as a unity principle integrating all experiences.

Whichever way you look at it, 'consciousness' has come to occupy the centre stage especially in the modern world where knowledge is power and source of all values. The power of artificial intelligence enhances human intelligence and offers the prospect of creating a network of enormously intelligent centres. Hence, consciousness, intelligence, information and knowledge have become the focus of study and research.

■ Can there be a basic definition for consciousness?

Consciousness can be defined through negation or in terms of its expressions. According to the Indian philosophers consciousness is the factor that makes experience possible but itself is not an object of experience. Another idea of consciousness is that it is the raw material and source of everything. The third idea is that it is the infinite inexhaustible energy. It is invisible, but the very substance of the subject.

I doubt whether consciousness can be ever seen under the microscope, or is amenable for measurement and manipulation for partisan human ends. But I strongly believe that consciousness can manifest as intelligence, energy and health, which constitute the sense of wellness of human beings. These manifestations are available for measurement and objective experience. The pursuit of knowledge being endless, consciousness will be an ever-eluding phenomenon unwilling to reveal all her faces and depths to limited and greed-based human investigations.

This does not mean that one should not try to understand consciousness through neurobiological studies and creation of artificial intelligence and also by probing into subjective consciousness through *Yogic* and other disciplines.

■ What is the *Vedāntic* approach to consciousness?

The *Vedāntic* approach to consciousness is that consciousness is the source of everything. *Vedānta* reduces the subject-object duality involved in any experience into consciousness. Consciousness is not opposed to the conscious and unconscious, is beyond both, and accommodates the objective and subjective. *Vedānta* prescribes the path of discernment, negation and detachment to realise identity with consciousness.

***Vedānta* reduces the subject-object duality involved in any experience into consciousness.**

I am not totally happy with this prescription. I think that it is a partial methodology. We have to incorporate the modern methods and research findings into the understanding of consciousness, which will make the *Vedāntin's* understanding of consciousness rich and the scientist's understanding of consciousness deep.

■ There are two issues highlighted in much of the current discussions on consciousness: namely 'where is consciousness' (its locality), and 'why quantitative and local phenomena (neural processes) give rise to qualitative subjective experiences'.

Firstly, consciousness cannot be located – limited by space. That does not mean it cannot be invoked through a localised process. I would like to cite the metaphor of a television reception set. It is able to receive the electronic signals telecast from the television station. But what the receiving set processes and brings out as colour and sound are not sourced from the receiving set. Similarly, a localised process like neural firing is capable of receiving and processing data and manifesting consciousness. If consciousness is the source of everything even the neurobiological processes have to be sourced into consciousness.

Therefore it is possible for a localised phenomenon being capable of accessing non-localised data and information.

- Artificial systems can emulate conscious behaviour, according to the ongoing research, and can be intelligent or emotional, at least to certain degrees, as we human beings are.

I have two ideas on this subject. One is that even if you can mimic conscious behaviour and pretend that there is a conscious subject that experiences, I do not believe that this would give the full story of consciousness apart from exhibiting the phenomenal characteristics of an experience. A conscious experiencer can never be mimicked. Consciousness is a unique phenomenon and is not available for replication.

A conscious experiencer can never be mimicked.

On the other side, as technology gains sufficient sophistication, artificial intelligence people might be able to expand the mental and sensory faculties of individual subjects and create a man–machine synergy. We may also be able to develop networks and enough database to create unique individual machines and new versions of subjective realities. These virtual subjective realities may appear to have identities without any deep subjective experience.

- Perhaps, in the coming century of research, the phenomenon would lose the 'mysticism' and 'ephemerality' bestowed on it through centuries, and will be available for manipulation, control and prediction like any other physical phenomenon.

It is possible to gain greater understanding and control of what is unknown of consciousness today. But as we approach the problem and conquer new continents of the problem, we still would find the mystery deepening. It is a situation where, the more we expand our area of knowledge the more our area of ignorance also will expand. I definitely believe that we would be able to catch the tail of consciousness with more and more research.

The more we expand our area of knowledge the more our area of ignorance also will expand.

An important question that arises is what do we expect to gain from this research. Is it how to control human behaviour, is it how to understand human intelligence, is it to know the source of everything, or is it to create conscious beings? I feel that we are not clear about the goals to be achieved by the study of consciousness.

- An interesting discussion is centred on the two functions of consciousness, such as, the ability to gain knowledge and to know of that knowledge. These issues:

  i. I know,

  ii. I know that I know, and,

  iii. I know that you know that I know,

  were taken by Dennett in a biological and reductionistic analysis of intelligence that included animal intelligence also in it by proposing degrees of intentionality.

Consciousness, as I understand, is an inherent faculty in all life forms from the unicellular amoebae to the most developed human brain. Consciousness is ubiquitous and universal. Its expression may vary depending upon the complexity of the neural system. The idea of consciousness includes all physical patterns and formations. All life forms are networks of information. Information is a mode of consciousness. From this standpoint all manifestations are expressions of consciousness.

Discussions about intentionality and 'knowledge about knowledge' have their echo in the *Vedāntic* literature. It is possible to go backward *ad infinitum*. The difference lies in the ontological concept of consciousness. As you said, if consciousness can be reduced to biological processes and the biological to physical processes, you eliminate the independent and ontological status of consciousness.

Our understanding of the physical process has to change as is happening in quantum physics where it tends to reduce physical processes into vibrating 'strings' whose impulse is intentional and conscious. The ability 'to know', and 'to know that one knows', and 'to know the knowing self' are all different functions of the same consciousness.

There are three fundamental questions: Is consciousness ontologically primary or secondary? Is cognition a function of consciousness or a neural process? Is experience subjective or a result of the interplay of objects? I do not say that these questions can be answered fully by any scientist or philosopher or spiritualist. But posing these questions could avoid the pitfall of reductionism and help the research to go deep into the heart of the problem.

■ 'Self-awareness' is a function which is taken as the test for measuring the degree of consciousness in animals. What are the philosophical implications of 'self-awareness' and the difference, if any, from a biological approach to the same?

The biological approach to consciousness seems to me is more reductionistic than holistic and more behavioural than ontological. Biological approach limits the scope and definition of enquiry unlike the philosophical approach. But, at the same time, the biological approach is a necessary component in the enquiry into consciousness since it helps remove a lot of verbal cobwebs and superstitious ideas held by spiritualists and philosophers.

The ontological approach to consciousness is a necessary corrective to the neurobiological approach.

The ontological approach to consciousness is a necessary corrective to the neurobiological approach. The neurobiological approach is a necessary corrective to the imaginary and untested ideas of romantics in the field of consciousness studies.

■ Can a non-human physical system be made conscious by emulating human neural processes? Or do you think that 'consciousness' as encountered/ experienced by a human is qualitatively different?

A physical system can be created which can emulate all conscious behaviour of a human being if there are enough data to design a software. But I doubt whether the conscious experience of the subject can be created *ab nihilo*. You may be able to separate a cell and let it grow in an environment that is conducive and nourish an individual. But to assemble a full-fledged individual out of prefabricated parts seems to be a wrong methodology and betrays lack of understanding of subjective consciousness that is indivisible and non-created.

These are my provisional thoughts. From another standpoint it seems that if we can create an appropriate material configuration then we will indeed be able to trap a mind and manifest consciousness and create conscious subjective realities and experiences. All said and done it is a praiseworthy endeavour of the scientist to put together a subjective, experiencing individual.

- Is the self which experiences one single experience at any given moment (e.g. 'I am happy'), and the self which is aware of the entire gamut of experiences it had, has or will have, are two degrees of consciousness? How would you see the complexity involved here?

A living experience, an experience of the moment, is different from a dead experience.

A living experience, an experience of the moment, is different from a dead experience. An experience of the past which has come and gone remains only as a memory. Since memory and its recall require an enduring subject, there is identity of the experiencer and the recaller. One can safely presume that the identity of both, the one who experiences the moment's events and one who recalls the past experiences, compares and judges them, is the same. The entire past of the experiencing self is involved in an experience of the moment.

Otherwise the phenomena of recalling, comparing, judging, creating values and meanings and having a sense of fulfillment are not possible.

■ Can one really have an objective understanding of consciousness?

I increasingly tend to discount the importance of dividing reality into objective and subjective parts. With reference to mind, sensations are objective. But mind itself becomes objective with reference to seeing (seeing is just perception prior to conception and comprehension) consciousness which itself becomes objective with reference to knowing consciousness which in turn becomes objective with reference to pure consciousness. Therefore I think that there is a lot of scope for the objective study of consciousness.

One should not discourage research into consciousness because objective parameters are employed. Perhaps in the modern world that is all we can do as people have lost the capacity for any other mode of investigation.

■ Knowledge as well as experience seem to be key factors in order to understand the conscious being as well as consciousness in the area of artificial intelligence as well as neurobiological research. Are 'knowledge' and 'experience' really different, though knowledge can be objectified to a larger extent than experience which is more an immediate event than a process?

Actually they are two sides of the same coin. Knowledge is processed experience that in turn influences the content and quality of experience. Their mutual interaction has a spiraling effect leading to higher levels of knowledge and experience. When I see a flower, that simple encounter involves knowledge and experience. 'Seeing' is both knowledge and experience. When I reflect on the experience I am able to create secondary levels of knowledge that influences my understanding of the primary experience and the subsequent experiences of the flower.

In the strict sense I feel that knowledge and experience are the two faces of the same process. One can imagine situations of verbal knowledge without the experience of the object, or a somnambulistic experience of the object without the knowledge of experiencing it. It is something like when I look for a certain object I may see it but do not recognise it and as a result miss it. It all depends upon the context that we refer to when we analyse knowledge, experience and their relationship.

■ It is amazing that though we live in at least three different kinds of worlds – waking, dream and deep sleep – where the object and means of experience are totally different we still see a coherence between all three and seem to have an experiential consensus about the waking state. The waking state seems to have a larger reality, since my physical body corresponds to it. We also are structured in such a way that we 'comfortably accept' the time and space in the waking state to be real and natural, when we very well know that this time and space does not hold good in the dream and deep sleep state. Can we have an experience which is unconditioned by time and space which we are 'familiar' with?

No! Only time–space events can become objects of experience. An experience that is not conditioned by time and space is a realisation where the subject does not brood over the experience, but transcends both the object and subject of experience, where time and space evaporate and only the flame of ecstasy remains. This experience does not become memory since it will not be sublated by any further experience. In fact this is the only abiding experience that Krishnamurthi calls 'objectless consciousness' and Śankarācārya calls 'mediumless experience' (*aparokṣa anubhūti*).

I started this answer by responding 'No' to your proposition. But I would like to conclude the answer by a resounding 'Yes'.

■ What are your views on the article in the recent issue of *Newsweek* on 'neurotheology' tracing religious experiences of 'losing the sense of self' or ' feeling one with the universe' etc. to distinct firings in specific cortical areas. Does religious experience ultimately mean 'distinct nature and function of brain processes' which might be repicated in laboratory conditions?

Spiritual experiences can have neural correlates. At the same time, they are not products of neural firings.

Spiritual experiences can have neural correlates. At the same time, they are not products of neural firings.

In the Indian tradition there is *kuṇḍalini śāstra* which talks about nourishing the brain conserving sexual energy, by controlling negative emotions like anger, greed, lust and opening up the full potential of the neural system and reaching cosmic experiences.

I firmly believe that correlations are possible, but spiritual experiences cannot be reduced to neural processes nor can be created by stimulating or simulating neural firings and processes. It is something like one can think of sugar and salivate but that will not be the true experience of sugar.

- Can we understand 'consciousness' as a phenomenon keeping it apart from its religious and biological implications?

Let me understand the spirit of this question. What you mean might be that the spiritual and biological understanding of consciousness is not complete; or that consciousness as a phenomenon is different from the spiritual and biological. I believe that consciousness being the source of everything has a spiritual and biological content in its fullness.

- I experience the world when my sense organs are 'opened' and the world 'disappears' when my sense organs operate no more. Is the world which I experience, so much connected and related to my physical and mental consciousness?

If the question implies that the world is a creation of the senses and the mind, the answer is 'no'. The world is as much real as the senses and mind are. If the question indicates that the mind and senses interact with the world in creating experiences and realities for the experiencer, the answer is 'yes'.

- How do you distinguish between body, mind and consciousness?

The body–mind complex and its processes are objects of consciousness and ever changing, whereas consciousness is ever the subject and never changes. The body–mind has existence with reference to consciousness while consciousness exists without reference to it.

- Without the body, I cannot experience and interact. Without the mind I cannot have possible imagination and ideas to choreograph my experiences and exchanges. Where and what is this 'I' which is so elusive and still commands so much?

Since 'I' is not an object of experience it remains ever elusive. Its existence is understood in deep silence or as the reality behind the shadow of ever changing experiences. It is partly known by inference, partly known by a deep sense of its existence, and partly known by an insight caused by the crisis of the ever-changing nature of experiences.

- In order to create physical objects and have ideas, I have to use time–space and incorporate causal principles. But what does consciousness use as its tool to create this universe of time–space causal experiences and events, make possible its appearance and disappearance, and so too make it so natural and given and not 'created'?

You use the expression 'I' with reference to the experience of time-space and causal events. It is the same 'I' that refers to consciousness. Instead of using the word 'I' you may as well use the word 'consciousness'. Consciousness, being infinite information, is the creator of time, space and causal events.

- Do you think that 'pure consciousness' is an abstract concept which helps us to integrate and holistically view varied experiences? May be there is no 'consciousness' without the body and the mind!

It is the reality of the experiencer, consciousness is an abstract concept to understand experiences for a logical thinker. For a realised individual, for a meditative thinker, it is the only reality.

- Body and bodily interactions and exchanges constitute a larger part of human lives. At the same time many of us would like to think that by itself the body is just a dead physical apparatus. It is once again amazing that the utility value of the body is so much that there is no sensible world of interaction and exchange without it, at the same time, we are continuously engaged in thinking/understanding the cause of physical life and the otherness of it beyond physical birth and death.

This is one of the paradoxes in human life that, as an object of thought, body is very flimsy, fleeting and infinitesimal. But any thought is possible only when the body is intact and alive. The dance between body and consciousness, the finite and infinite, is one of the mysteries of human experience.

A time may come when we will be able to transfer consciousness and memory from brain to an artificial system. And, perhaps by then we may not even require a physical system for preserving memory and experiences. Ultimately intelligence must be able to function without a medium or with minimal intervention.

Ultimately intelligence must be able to function without a medium or with minimal intervention.

These are areas that one could investigate. For me, since everything is a modification of consciousness, I do not see a qualitative difference between mind, body and material objects. They are all manifestations infused with consciousness or they are all manifestations of consciousness. Whichever object you take for investigation, whether it is a piece of stone, neuron, a thought, a feeling, a photon or an atom you have to reach the same smiling face of consciousness.

■ What are your views or suggestions towards research in consciousness studies?

As I suggested earlier, the neurobiological stream, quantum mechanical stream, artificial intelligence stream, networking of computers, search for extraterrestrial intelligence in the outer space, genome mapping, peoples' efforts to watch themselves and practice psychophysical disciplines – must all go hand in hand toward the great hunt for consciousness or 'god' or 'unified field' or 'theory of everything'. That is my idea of search for consciousness.

Consciousness cannot be discovered singly by any one of these pursuits. I also believe that the blessings of consciousness can be invoked and experienced incessantly by a meditative mind engaged in an interactive life with self-giving intent and without self-aggrandising motives. Through self-giving activities one could invoke infinite intelligence and energies of consciousness and realise its infinite potentialities. That will be God-realisation and that will be the final reward of consciousness studies.

4

Lifestyles and Value Systems

■ Are there various ways of responding to specific situations?

Yes! Being creative, intelligence devises many ways of responding to situations. However these variations in responses are, to certain extent, conditioned by the nature of the situation. There is a mutually conditioning influence between a situation and the response.

■ What, according to you, designs the lifestyle of an individual?

The lifestyle of an individual is determined by the geographic and climatic conditions, creativity of the society he lives in, interactions with different cultures, the worldview of the community to which he belongs, the availability of resources and the nature of his needs – psychological, physical and aesthetic – that he has developed over a period of time. To sum up, the lifestyle of an individual is designed by his survival needs, both as a physical and psychological being.

■ What is a value? What is the importance of values?

Value is something tangible or intangible that you see in an object, person or situation which can give you, the value-holder, satisfaction and the sense of wellbeing that can enhance your survival and growth. The individual makes a sacrifice to attain that value and that sacrifice can be the measure of the value that he seeks to attain. When you pay ten rupees for a kilogram of sugar you measure the value of sugar in terms of rupees. There may be some parity between the labour you put in to earn ten rupees and the satisfaction that a kilogram of sugar gives you. When a culture insists on the postponement of immediate gratification for the sake of the greater long term good of the individual, like study instead of play, developing skills instead of indulgence, the individual is asked to pay a price by making a sacrifice now for a greater gain later which will be more rewarding than the sacrifices he makes.

The end value is the integrity of the individual.

Value can be understood in terms of what you get and what you give in exchange. It could mean physical or mental discipline, anything that can enhance your life. The end value is the integrity of the individual. Any sacrifice the individual makes to attain the end value can be called instrumental value.

■ Though the applications and particular references of values would be different across global cultures and communities, humanity as a whole finds value systems important factors in guiding their behaviour and organising their activities.

I agree with this presentation that nuances of values can change across cultures but no system can survive without values in terms of worthy goals and means for attaining those goals. An assimilated system of values is absolutely necessary for organising life in a world of self-seeking individuals trying to maximise their happiness.

- With the development of science and technology possibilities for more and more comforts and sophistication also emerge. With indulgence in more and more products of comforts, there is on one side the decadence of values and regard for uniqueness. For example, the IT revolution in India and, probably the rest of the world, has resulted in computerisation of much of what we would like to call engagements with a human touch. What used to bear the simple and innocent human touch is replaced by the no-face computer. Emails have almost taken away the beauty of reading the loved one's letters in his/her own hand. On the other hand technology reduces our uncertainties and increases efficiency and faster communication, all leading to better creation and sharing of information. But in this fast ride are not we leaving behind so much of what is called the 'human face and touch'?

Science and technology have come here to stay and they interpose themselves between humans and nature and change our realities. You have looked only at one aspect of technological revolution: the loss of intimacy and human touch. On the other hand, it has brought peoples together. It has made it possible for people of distant lands and cultures to communicate. It has extended the scope of human consciousness. It has increased the reach of human compassion. When thousands perished in the recent Gujarat earthquake, the whole world came to know about it almost instantly and was able to rush to the help of the unfortunate victims.

Science and technology have liberated humankind from the drudgery of daily chores and made comforts earlier enjoyed by a few available universally. Internet and computer facilities may help people to reach each other instantly rather than wait impatiently for the loved one's letters for days and weeks. I do not think that science and technology have made humans less human, or less the lovers of nature. A recent picture published in daily, *Times of India*, testified to this fact: the entire traffic on a busy Canadian highway coming to a grinding halt because of a duck and its ducklings crossing the highway.

I believe in the liberating and humanising power of science an technology.

All these indicate technology and human intelligence jointly reaching to higher levels of life. We may be forced to leave cherished lifestyles but we are emerging into what might be much more cherished. I believe in the liberating and humanising power of science and technology.

- What is your view on India's political and religious history that might have also directed the visions, views and lifestyles of the people of this nation?

I find the history of India in the last 1500 years very upsetting and humiliating. Such a grand civilisation, which is the oldest; a country which is most populous; and with rich literature like the *Mahābhārata*, *Rāmāyana*, *Upaniṣads*, *Bhagavad Gītā* and *Vedās*, *Manusmṛti*, *Arthaśāstra*, *Yogasutrās* and the *Aṣṭādhyāyi* grammar rules of Panini; highly advanced in mathematics, astronomy and medicine, comes to live under foreigners seems to be the greatest mystery of history.

Either India ran out of steam in the 4th or 5th century after the Guptas, or there was something radically wrong in our spiritual philosophies, our worldviews, and sociopolitical institutions that we built based on those worldviews. I remember reading *Discovery of India*, where similar questions were raised. Nehru's answer was that India's technological backwardness and lack of social coherence were the main reasons for her downfall. At the same time India survived, if not as a geopolitical unity, but as a concept and a civilisation, and is still flourishing with new institutional frameworks like parliamentary democracy, universal suffrage and the concept of an egalitarian society and rule of law.

It is a very confusing and frustrating situation, that India as a nation has vital and critical strengths but at the same time shows infuriating weaknesses impeding purposeful action. It is not possible for one individual to understand and respond to these complex situations. My hope is that democracy and market forces networking to the global economy will transform India into a very vibrant civilisation, learning from and contributing to other cultures and civilisations.

■ Are political forces a major influence in framing the psyche of the people of a nation?

Politicians and political forces, especially in a democracy, reflect and represent the economic forces that operate in the society. I strongly believe that economics plays a big role in shaping society's responses to situations.

Of course politicians can provide leadership to organise and direct these forces. But they cannot create the forces over which they preside. Good political decisions have to be good economic decisions. But the problem in our country is that good economic decisions are not always good political decisions. Because, the majority of our people are still poor and have no means of making choices for themselves and hence are dependent on the government and assistance from the state. This creates a parasitic society where the majority does not proportionately contribute to national wealth but demands a higher share and thus creates an economy of inefficiency, deceit and greed.

By timely political interventions this situation can be corrected. But unless the economy gains a critical mass politicians will not dare to take such bold decisions. It is a vicious cycle, provoking the proverbial question 'who will bell the cat'? People get the rulers they deserve: *yathā prajā tathā rājā*!

- Can we remove corruption at global and individual levels?

Corruption will end when the citizens are educated, when they have a say in the creation and distribution of wealth and have a stake in a clean and honest government. As long as the people remain poor nobody can be free from the temptation to make a few fast bucks using his official influence and proximity to political power.

The best way to remove corruption is to liberalise, privatise and globalise. But I am not sure whether this will work in an abysmally poor country like India unless we create the critical mass of the middle-class that can influence public opinion and government policies. Till such time corruption will continue. It is a way for the poor society to survive, by deceit and corruption.

The best way to remove corruption is to liberalise, privatise and globalise.

- With liberalisation, Indian media has welcomed satellite channels, much of which relays second quality content. A major outcome of this is its influence on the growing minds which find an alternative to follow and grow up with the label 'western or modern trends and styles'.

If we respect Western societies for their wealth, standard of living, individual rights, rule of law and their science and technology, I do not see how we can separate their Coca-Cola, jeans, Kentucky fried chicken, potato chips, Hollywood movies and ruthless individualistic values. There is a reverse flow too with the West being influenced by Eastern family values, spiritualism, medicine and the holistic way of looking at life.

I think our youth should be exposed to everything: good and bad, but at the same time develop skills to differentiate between what is healthy and unhealthy, and develop habits and character to choose the healthy and avoid the unhealthy. It is not by ignorance and denial that one cultivates character. It is by developing the power of the intellect and the knowledge to choose the good and the noble that one nurtures healthy individuals and builds a nation.

I believe in the free flow of ideas, lifestyles and values.

I believe in the free flow of ideas, lifestyles and values. Let every individual become a light unto oneself and choose his/her values according to his/her judgment and become responsible for his/her own destiny.

■ Is it possible to change lifestyles and have total reorientation of our value systems?

It is possible to change. That is what has happened to the Western society for the last 500 years. There, the scientific temper, democratic impulses, the concept of a civil society and rule of law are becoming universal values. That was a radical departure from the values of medieval societies. At the same time you find old values persisting in poorer, as well as in populous Eastern countries. What you find is both continuities and discontinuities, and that is how societies progress.

■ What is *Puruṣartha*?

Four cardinal values in a hierarchical order are laid out for human deliberation and action.

Puruṣārtha literally means human goals, meaning values pursued by human beings as choice makers. Four cardinal values in a hierarchical order are laid out for human deliberation and action. They are not artificially imposed but are derived from natural human impulses. These values are: first, biological needs like food, sex and shelter; second, security needs like money and possessions; third, the need for love, respect, community and coexistence values like non-violence and truthfulness; fourth, spiritual values like freedom and self actualisation. The Sanskrit terms for these are *kāma, artha, dharma* and *mokṣa*.

These are not unrelated values. Individuals are primarily concerned with creature needs and then security needs. But since they have to pursue these goals within the society made of people pursuing similar needs, they have to restrain their impulses and conform to socially accepted rules of conduct in the pursuit of private goals. When all these needs are fulfilled then the human is ready for pursuing the ultimate goal of freedom or self-realisation.

I find the hierarchy of values propounded by Abraham Maslow in his book *Psychology of Being* bearing similarity to this Hindu concept of human needs and goals. Since Maslow came much later than the times of the *Gītā* and *Manusmṛti*, I feel that Maslow should have acknowledged the existence of this knowledge system in the Eastern society. Since he has not done it, and since I cannot question his honesty and integrity, I can only assume that he was ignorant of world thought and he is the poorer for that.

■ How can we at the same time have ideals for desire (*kāma*) and liberation from all desires (*mokṣa*); and create wealth (*artha*) and have equity and fair deals (*dharma*)?

I do not believe that these are contradictory values: desire and desirelessness, or desire for comforts and desire for freedom; similarly creation of wealth, equity, justice and fairness. In fact, the desire for the other is the desire to expand and accommodate the dissimilar. Desire for comforts is the legitimate need of the complex organism that requires an environment that is conducive for survival. Desire for freedom, or desirelessness, is actually the desire to unfold one's potential and the desire to capture and realise one's nature as unconditional happiness.

Desire is the very impulse of life. To suppress or ignore desire is suicidal and a sure way to neurosis and disease.

Desire is the very impulse of life. To suppress or ignore desire is suicidal and a sure way to neurosis and disease. Even *Brahman* desires to become many and to realise the hidden potential. Actually, it is not desire which inhibits human freedom, but rather the reaction to the outcome of the desired project which inhibits self-expression.

I would define freedom as progressive realisation of worthy goals in an ever-unfolding experience of inner energies. So too, social equity, justice and fairness require wealth of consumable goods and services. One has to think of wealth creation before wealth distribution. The old idea that an individual becomes wealthy at the cost of other individuals is no longer valid. We are living in a world where an individual's wealth-creating ability synergistically depends upon other individuals' wealth-creating abilities and activities.

To grow is to grow together.

To grow is to grow together. That is the meaning of competition, international trade and a market economy. That is the experience of South Asian tiger nations. By integrating with world economy and by international trade they raised their per capita income to unprecedented levels.

I repeat, creation of wealth is a necessary precondition for distribution of wealth and equity. Otherwise what you distribute will be only ignorance, poverty and disease.

■ How do we understand the increase of violence, and the increase of nonviolent spiritual or religious movements, globally? Is it an unconscious attempt to create more opportunities for washing away the increasing number of sins we commit?

As long as resources are limited and individuals pursue their individual agenda, there will be desire to control resources and people, and the resultant violence. Violence will end only when people find cooperation and nonviolence economically more productive and individually more favourable to the advancement of personal achievements.

Violence, that is control over another, in favour of the controller rather than the controlled, is a law of nature – the big fish eating the small fish – *matsya nyāya*. It is by forming alliances and pressure groups and the networking of similarly situated individuals that such violence can be counter-balanced, which is the mode of functioning in a democratic pluralistic society.

I see violence and nonviolence more in terms of social dynamics than in terms of spirituality or religion, because we find that more people have died violent deaths in the name of god and religion than for any other cause. Those sages who have renounced violence out of unconditional love being so insignificantly few has no practical influence on humanity's behaviour – either in the recrudescene of violence or in the flowering of cooperation.

■ More middle class and upper middle class Indian families today face a major challenge, which is the deterioration of values and identity crises facing their children. How do you think we can cope with the excitement of cultural exchanges and technological advancements while at the same time preserving the depth of enduring and uniting values.

All cultures look for enduring and uniting values notwithstanding whether they are developed or developing societies. It is not science, technology or industrialisation alone that is to be blamed for violence or deterioration of values. If you read history you find even Socrates bemoaning the deterioration of values in his society and Socrates' detractors blaming him for the deterioration of values among the youth. I find that most of these criticisms are mere gossip and purely based on individual prejudices. It is like saying that the 'Yamuna is polluted' or the streets are littered while the complainant himself tosses litter into the rivers and on the roads. Doomsday sayers have always been there. And they always have been proved wrong.

All cultures look for enduring and uniting values notwithstanding whether they are developed or developing societies.

I find that Western society is very hard working, open minded, egalitarian, and creative and has a high respect for the individual, his dignity and his fundamental rights. Whereas Eastern societies, though they retain family, caste and community values, are highly irresponsible when it comes to civil communities, social assets and the rule of law. They have not eradicated poverty and do not find it uncomfortable to sustain an ostentatious lifestyle for a few in the midst of squalor and poverty. Those so-called cultural policemen who try to protect their native cultures and values are often champions and beneficiaries of old decadent societies. As long as poverty and poor people remain they will be strutting about.

What is needed is an integration of the world communities at all levels, learning from one another and creating a global society where individual rights are respected and individuals are given total freedom to make choices in pursuit of their goals.

■ Perhaps it is because of our inability to adjust to and absorb sudden and fast changes, I think, that our values are becoming more of double standards, and our personalities ruled by hypocrisies, psychological disruptions and perversions. Many of the so-called classical values and emotions are losing their charm and sacredness. Do love, trust, dedication, commitment etc. hold in as pristine a manner as in previous times?

I completely agree with the first part of your statement, that our inability to participate and learn and contribute to the knowledge and value creating enterprise of the world makes us paranoid and forces us to cling to old values and lifestyles. At the same time, our secret respect for that which we oppose publicly makes us speak in 'double tongues', and, we become hypocrites.

The real source of values is the consciousness of a free, fearless and choice-making individual.

In India we find the greatest champions of *svadeśi* in their political wilderness becoming the staunchest champions of *videśi* when they come to power. Whereas nourishing values, which have enduring relevance anywhere in the world at any stage of economic development, such as love, trust, hard work and sharing will continue to be respected, practiced and propagated. I see that these values are more in practice in a developed, law-abiding society rather than in a traditional, corrupt society.

The real source of values is the consciousness of a free, fearless and choice-making individual.

■ What is the meaning of the classical description of reality as *satyaṃ*, *śivaṃ*, and *sundaraṃ?*

These are the three end values that humans seek to realise in their life. In the Western knowledge system the discipline of logic pursues the ideal of truth, ethics pursues the ideal of goodness and aesthetics pursues the ideal of beauty. But still in the Western mind they remain objective, sensate, logical and social values, one different from the other, whereas for the Indian mind these are subjective, transcendent, non-logical and experiential values which the individual realises when the mind is pure and gets access to the all-encompassing transcendent reality.

■ Can ancient cultures and modern technologies go hand in hand in creating and preserving well-founded communities and civilisations?

It depends upon the choice of individuals and communities.

How many people would like to live in forests, sleep under the trees, in the caves, drinking water from running brooks, eating roots and leaves, chasing rats and in constant fear of wild animals? How many of us will be willing to live in large joint families with uncles, granduncles, grandmothers, mothers-in-law and all kinds of sundry relatives breathing heavily down our necks? How many would like to share their hard-earned income with unemployed and unemployable lazy nephews and uncles in an extended family? How many will be ready to live on an isolated farm sowing and harvesting their own produce or in a self-sufficient village community without travelling in aeroplanes and vacationing on exotic islands? How many can live without cars and roads, televisions, refrigerators and washing machines? How will you create a strong nation based on self-sufficient village communities on the lines of Gandhiji's Hindu *Svarāj*?

I do not understand, what it is meant by preserving primitive and native cultures unless they are meant for museums or are maintained as exotic preserves. I would like a realistic, enlightened and learned dialogue between champions of native cultures, leaders of native communities and votaries of industrial civilisation. Such a dialogue will help concerned individuals to make their own choices. In the modern world of travel, instant communication and global markets with a high degree of interdependence, it is impossible to preserve native communities, primitive societies, languages, customs and traditions.

What is required is a globally integrated community of individuals.

What is required is a globally integrated community of individuals. This does not mean everybody should dress and behave uniformly. People can be creative in their lifestyles drawing from their past and other cultures. But any attempt to preserve native cultures and lock them into old customs and lifestyles will not be successful and is not fair. I believe in the dictum, 'let noble thoughts come from all sides'. Let the end user decide what he wants. Give him information, empower him and let him decide.

■ How can I help myself to make a choice between what is desirable and what is enduring for me in a given situation?

Each one of us has our own inner standards of what is desirable and what is not desirable. We also know what we want and when we want it. If a person has not cultivated that inner standard, then he is an uneducated barbarian. A cultivated person becomes a responsible citizen in the society sensitive to the inalienable and inviolable rights and needs of others.

The purpose of education is to activate and cultivate this inner faculty, and inculcate well-understood and assimilated value systems, which we call character-building education. This education is accomplished by studying and reflecting on the collective wisdom tradition of the race and the community, the collectively agreed law of the land, and observing and learning from other people of integrity and character and watching one's own needs and expectations. I think that in this complex world of massive exchange of information and data, every individual is uniquely situated and each individual is responsible for constructing his/her own value system. Others can only challenge you. Nobody

Let the end user decide what he wants.

can teach or become an absolute guide for anybody else. Since the world is moving so fast, nobody is privy to privileged information. The old dictum of Buddha 'to be a light unto yourself' is relevant in this context too.

- **Caste is an eternal factor for India's underdevelopment and its complex social structure. What is your view on caste and *cāturvarṇya*?**

Cāturvarṇya, or the division of the society into four *varṇās* or categories as knowledge seekers, power seekers, money seekers and creature comfort seekers seems to be scientific. But when the criterion of this division is by the fact of birth it makes a travesty of this scientific law. One has to have more scientific and practical criteria for classifying people into these types. So too, caste which was a nonviolent way of accommodating dissimilar people and cultures, practicing different crafts and trades became so fossilised that the talent pool available in a particular caste shrank. Because again the criterion was based on birth, and hence new talents did not come into the trade.

What is necessary is to take away the criterion of birth in deciding *varṇa* and caste and let the individual by his proven abilities and dispositions through an open system of competition prove his competence. If that happens then Indian society will break out of the caste and *varṇa* mode based on birth, and without giving up the scientific advantage of such a division, we will be able to reorganise our society into a dynamically interacting, learning and achieving community.

The criterion of birth was a valuable instrument in a traditional society where the centre of activity was the family and the small community. The father taught the skills to the son in the verandah of his house. Now children do not learn skills from parents. Even at the age of three they go to schools and they travel to far off countries to learn new knowledge. In such a fluid system, only through open competition can one know and prove which *varṇa* and caste he belongs to.

A society that is governed by a team of meritorious people, who reach the top through the process of competition alone, can become a successful and creative society.

■ Can Indian polity be value-based?

I sympathise with the sentiment of that question. If value is defined in a narrow sense of ethical and moral imperatives, without regard to economic and social realities, and by making our standards of values stringent and one-dimensional, which is advantageous to the existing power structure, then I do not think we will have value-based politics. Often corruption occurs in politics, government, or industry because of the stringent controls and unintelligent policies followed by the government that constrict and restrict the creative impulses of the people. In a free and prosperous society, where every citizen is conscious of his rights and takes responsibility for his destiny, there will be very little corruption and social interaction and governance based on trust and transparency will follow.

- How can we as global communities integrate the impact of modernity on traditions in the context of our need for social, economic and political changes leading to more development and better foundation, as a civilisation?

By intelligently understanding the value of traditional lifestyles, their enhancing and inhibiting aspects, one can successfully integrate tradition into modern society. Modern society is not an all-devouring monster. It preserves what is healthy in tradition and discards what is unhealthy. In fact we find that in the globalised village, traditional life styles are also globalised, uniqueness and dissimilarities are celebrated.

Traditional cultures do not have to fear the global culture. Global culture is a celebration of the plurality of cultures. A global citizen is a tolerant and accommodating individual. Even in religious fields the global citizen accepts all religions as his religion, all cultures as his culture.

Traditional cultures do not have to fear the global culture.

The characteristic features of global culture are tolerance and accommodation. Global culture is not a colonising and proselytizing culture but is the culture that celebrates uniqueness and plurality.

- Is there an ideal lifestyle? Is there an ultimate value?

There are as many ideal lifestyles, as many values, as many goals as there are people. But I think two values are universal. One is respect for the other which I call nonviolence, or love or tolerance, and the other is transparency, which I would call truthfulness, honesty, openness, humility and trust. These two values are foundational and universal values from which one can derive all other values.

As Veda Vyasa said *ahimsā paramo dharma* – nonviolence is the highest virtue; and the *Upaniṣad* declared, *satyaṃ eva jayate* – truth alone triumphs. The global community will be built on these two values.

5

Pain and Relationships

■ Physical and psychological pain is the unavoidable consequence of human living. What is your view on the prospect of finding an end to all kinds of pain?

Experience of pain is an insignia of life. Inert objects do not experience pain. Pain is a necessary condition of life. It monitors the environment and health of the living being. We may come to a state when pain can be avoided by genetic interventions, with the help of medicines or with advancements in brain research. But I do not think that such stoppage of pain will be helpful for a healthy life. Considering all aspects of the issue it seems that pain is a necessary ingredient of a sensitive life.

I feel that there are three kinds of pain – physical, philosophical, and psychological. Physical pain is a sign of health. A healthy person feels pain if his limbs are hurt, or a malign external agent enters into his system, or his inner organs for some reason do not function properly. In such cases pain is a kind of alarm system that alerts the body about the data. A person who suffers from leprosy may not feel pain when he is in contact with fire or sharp objects. But that is not healthy. We would invite pain in such situations rather than enjoy not having pain. When the body regains its original health the alarm becomes silent and the individual has no more pain. It is like when the house is on fire the alarm gets activated, so that effective preventive measures can be immediately undertaken.

Experience of pain is an insignia of life.

The second kind of pain is philosophical. When I see suffering, a child begging on the pavement, a pregnant woman crying for help, a disabled person crawling across the road unattended, an old woman thrown out of her house, a young woman raped, or when those who are custodians of peoples become perpetrators of crimes, then I feel pained. Not that it affects me physically. But it affects my sensitivity, my sense of wellness and I am pained to see such situations. I would call it a healthy pain, a healthy restlessness that calls for deliberation and action, which calls for empathy and sacrifice.

These two modes of pain are signs of a healthy body and a healthy mind. Unless we achieve great strides in the field of science and technology and bring the fruits of those achievements for the common man's benefit, and also achieve great improvements in the health sciences, a sensitive, healthy man will continue to have experiences of both physical and philosophical pain. I find no way of ending them.

The third kind of pain is psychological. It is mainly due to human interactions and expectations that govern such interactions. The fear of death, deprivation, comparison, humiliation, frustration and the disappointments and uncertainties of life's prospects: all these cause psychological pain. And mostly they are imaginary pains based upon previous freak experiences.

We can also call it ego-caused pain. If I suffer from cancer I have physical pain that I am able to undergo alone in my room. That physical pain is a tolerable and manageable pain. But the pain I feel when I look at my grieving wife, my innocent young children, my old widowed mother is an addition to, and is more unbearable than, the physical pain caused by the cancer tissues. When I start comparing myself to my neighbour or colleague who is quite healthy, it increases the acuteness of my pain. Comparing myself with my detractors, who secretly wish me ill and derive secret pleasure from my misfortunes, adds to the agony of my pain. That I will not be around to see my children going to college and that I will be leaving my widowed mother alone, and my wife unprotected, makes me further pained.

Psychological pain is very dissipating. It makes the individual weak, confused and clueless.

Similarly, humiliation, deprivation of desirable objects and association with unloved objects and people also cause pain. Psychological pain is very dissipating. It makes the individual weak, confused and clueless, whereas the earlier two modes of pain are healthy and expansive, and add to the quality of the individual's life.

Psychological pain can be avoided by the individual's intelligent efforts. Psychological pain can be ended by a philosophical approach to life and the other two pains by creative responses to the causes of those pains. The individual who is free from the exhausting struggles with psychological pain will have enough energy to creatively respond to his philosophical and physical pain.

This is how I understand the meaning of pain in human life.

■ I have a distinct identity and personality. Yet I interact with social institutions like family, work place etc. Why is it that though I have a distinct personality I have to live in a society which restrains me and controls me?

Your personality is not independent of the family, society and general environment where you live, work and grow. Therefore to live means to interact with your inner psyche and your outer environment each influencing the other. A healthy, learning and growing individual has to have a dynamically healthy relationship with his body and mind, his family, his work place and his society. I would also add that you must have a healthy worldview.

Your personality is not independent of the family, society and general environment where you live, work and grow.

This does not mean that the individual is just a product of his environment. The individual has enough initiative and freedom to learn from and contribute to the society in which he lives. One who lives in isolation from society will not be able to explore and express his full potential. So, I think a healthy individual is an interacting social animal.

■ Physical pain can be traced to specific physical causes and could have a medical explanation for it. But psychological pain is more complex. The same situation, event or person could be the cause of pain as well as happiness in different circumstances.

You are right. The cause of psychological pain is much more mysterious, deeper and complex than physical pain. I have a feeling that emotions like anger, jealousy, greed, arrogance etc. are acquired over a period of time, in the individual's struggle to survive as an entity. They do have an evolutionary purpose. They are primitive ways of alerting the individual against dangers to his survival. That is why they are so deeply entrenched.

The cause of psychological pain is much more mysterious, deeper and complex than physical pain.

I will not recommend a complete elimination of those impulses. What is called for is an intelligent way of controlling and using those emotions in our interactive lives because survival is the central concern and fundamental responsibility of any self-conscious system. By going into the very root of psychological pains one will be able to either eliminate them or understand their rationale and develop ways and disciplines to cope with them.

Psychological pain is a habit that was useful in a different set of circumstances and may not be useful in the new set of circumstances. Religious teaching says that the root of psychological pain is self-ignorance that manifests as desire, as greed to possess, to protect and to enjoy. But I would not go along all the way with such a diagnosis. Ignorance only means a narrow vision. Therefore, the vision has to be expanded. Desire can be converted into an expansive energy, greed into the ability to share and indulgence into creative self-expression. Instead of suppressing these energies, one has to organise their expression into healthy and positive channels. Psychological pain is a necessary part of the individual's psychic life; it has to be properly understood and channelled.

■ Having a mind is the cause of psychological pain. And, mind is a product of the culture we have built around. Can we do away with both mind and pain if we do away with culture?

Culture is defined as the language of 'do-s' and 'don't-s'. In an economy of limited resources and limitless desires one will not be able to do away with 'do-s' and 'don'ts'. The whole mind has been evolved in the scenario of limited resources and limitless aspirations.

Mind is essentially memory. If I have only one pen with me I must also remember where I keep it so that whenever I need it I can pick it up. If I have pens everywhere I do not have to remember where I keep one pen. Hence there is no need of memory. I do not see a situation in the mainstream life of humanity where culture, mind, memories and histories can be dispensed with. It may be possible for a few enlightened individuals who do not care for them, who live on the ground level of being, who live in spontaneity and who are free from culture, history and memory not to feel any kind of pain.

Pain is born of expectation. It is caused by the need to achieve goals and the necessity of making choices.

Pain is born of expectation. It is caused by the need to achieve goals and the necessity of making choices.

■ As an advanced civilisation we do science and build technologies for comfortable living. But at the same

> time, the maladies of human life such as death, disease, poverty etc. are prevalent without much change in kind over years. What is the primary role of an advanced civilisation through science and technology: to do away with maladies all together or create better comforts for a section of the society?

Death, disease and poverty are conditions of life. Life is very precious and rare in this vast universe. Living beings exist on this earth within a very limited space. The whole of nature is apparently trying to smother life. And that is the experience of death, disease and poverty. Life has to really struggle to exist in an extremely hostile environment. At the same time life is infinitely intelligent. Nature is like an ogress-mother. On one side it creates life and on the other eats life. When I look at the whole universe and the tiny human being and his tiny endeavours like reaching the moon or Jupiter in his flimsy spacecraft, I can only remember Einstein's statement that we are like children playing on the seashore with a handful of sand.

At the same time when I think about the power of consciousness and intelligence that encompasses the entire cosmos and processes information, and through imagination recreates this world, I become elated and excited. We may be able to overcome illnesses, poverty and even death either by technological innovations, or by redefining the meanings of these experiences, or by a quantum leap in the evolutionary process, or by interactions with extraterrestrial intelligence. But still the struggle between life and death will continue till the whole of existence becomes fully alive.

I believe that life is more enduring than death. Progress and evolution seem to be the course of nature that happens through selected and choice instruments. Hence the disparities between rich and poor, which are not just economical or intellectual but which covers the entire gamut of life, will continue.

I think progress is always through individuals and groups, and not as a whole.

I think progress is always through individuals and groups, and not as a whole. Disparities will continue in one form or the other. For example, the standard of life that an average citizen enjoys today is equivalent to the life of kings and chieftains of the old times. But that has not ended disparity in the modern world. In every successive stage of evolution there is going to be disparity.

- As a social being there is a social component to my life. As part of a family, I have family roles to play. As part of various institutions in society I have specific niches and functions. What am I really, the product of culture, societal institutions or evolutionary biology?

You are falling into the fallacy of reductionism. It has not worked in the physical sciences and much less in the social sciences, in psychology and understanding life as a whole. You are the glowing tip of existence, the growing part of life. You are the face of consciousness. And, you are the expression of the entire existence.

I would say that holistically an individual incorporates in his self the entire history of existence. For analytical purposes, you can pull apart the individual into social, biological, psychological and spiritual components but for living life integrally one has to have a holistic approach in which the rule is to unite and experience and not divide and gather knowledge.

- Human life is the interplay of pain, pleasure and relationships.

I agree with that beautiful proposition, that life is an interplay of pain, pleasure and relationships. I will also add that through this dynamics the individual learns and experiences the impulses of growth and self-expression. Pain and pleasure are two wheels of life that take you to the heart of your being. Relationships give you enough challenge to explore your potential. By this dialectical movement of pain and pleasure in an interactive life the individual reaches the mountaintop of ecstasy.

- Why is it that pain is not a universal phenomenon? The same situation which causes pain to me need not be a cause of worry for another. What is it that makes pain so individualistic?

The idiosyncratic nature of pain is because of the idiosyncrasy of the individual who interprets his experience. A simple explanation is that the quality, quantity and direction of the individual mind impacting upon the diverse world, which operates on the collective individual interests, often gets frustrated. This causes pain.

The individual's inability to order the world around him according to his needs causes psychological pain. But that does not mean that the individual should give up the effort to order the world according to his needs. Whereas along with attempts to order the world according to his needs he should also continue to evaluate his needs and update his needs according to his experience and knowledge.

The very fact that individuals are unique implies that their pains also are unique. The set of circumstances that cause pain to individual 'A' need not do so to individual 'B'.

- The human irony is that though he wants to avoid pain and unpredictable situations, he is hit with more pain. He is faced with more unpredictable situations, confusion in making decisions, regret over incorrect decisions made and having to face the present as well as the future over which he has no control.

I agree with your presentation of the human predicament. Uncertainties, anxieties and ironies are all part of the dynamic of life. The person who flows with the flow of life will be less subject to these problems and pains than a person who refuses to step in with the dance of life and lives in the memory of his bitter-sweet past.

I find that for one who is active and dynamic, every situation is a challenge rather than a reason for getting oppressed. What is poison for the overcautious is nectar for the enterprising.

- If relationships bring me pain, can I live without establishing various relationships in family, society etc.?

We have seen that pain is a necessary component of living. On second thought, I feel that pain is more life-engendering and life-expanding than pleasure. Pleasure is death. Pain is life. Pain is involved in any relationship. I do not support the religious view that pain can be completely eliminated by renouncing desire. By renouncing desire you may eliminate the pain impulse. But you also eliminate the opportunities and drive to step into uncertainties and the unknown by which one derives the maximum from life and experiences the true ecstasy of living. What is envisaged is a growing, flowering and pluralistic life where every individual finds his own unique way of fulfillment.

Pleasure is death. Pain is life.

Pain is involved in any relationship.

Desire is an important instrument for achieving ecstasy. Pain is the heart of life. I am not talking about the unnecessary psychological and egoistic pain. I am talking about the apprehensions of a new bride before she enters the bridal chamber, and the apprehension of a mother before she goes through the convulsions of childbirth. I am talking about the apprehensions of the daredevil before he jumps from the mountaintop. I am talking about the apprehensions of a pilot before he parachutes from the crashing plane. I am talking about the pain that fuels the fire of life.

■ Are not all our cultural, scientific and technological advancements the result of our deep and never ending feelings of insecurity?

Yes. I see some truth in what Freud said – that human civilisation is built upon the suppression of the pleasure principle. If all the Egyptians were happily married and settled there would not have been the pyramids. Nor would the Chinese wall have been built if the Chinese emperors had not conscripted free labour; nor the Taj Mahal if Shah Jahan did not extract work from his hapless citizens.

But I believe that a person with inner security will be more creative and active than a person with insecurity. An insecure society gives birth to a dictatorial command and control structure of governance whereas a secure society gives birth to a diffused, interactive and democratic frame of governance. Structures of control, governance and decision-making that we have in existence today are based upon the insecurity and fear principle. As people become more and more secure and self-confident, these structures will collapse giving rise to more open societies. In the modern world nobody thinks of building a pyramid or a Taj Mahal; that is purely an expression of vanity and arrogance of the ruling class. But we do think of a manned space shuttle landing on the moon, high rise buildings, transcontinental highways that arc supposedly more useful, and productive ways of enhancing civilisation.

I am sure that the landscape of human life will drastically change when people become more and more confident about themselves and centred in their being.

■ We, on the one hand, build objective knowledge systems and, on the other, are influenced by attitudes, emotional responses, personal whims and fancies of our mind. Is it not a contradiction that though we know the validity and stability of objective knowledge free from personal attributes, we always get entangled with a subjective world of relationships, duties and value systems which are highly personal and qualitative?

I think that life is a struggle between the objective and subjective. Subjective values and idiosyncratic aspirations that defy the logic of the objective world are a necessary component of life's dynamics. Life loves a crazy genius more than a classic law abiding citizen who is intimidated by objective facts. The physical laws of the universe should not be allowed to intimidate us or to smother our aspirations. That will be the death of life. The more we think differently and fly against physical laws and defy the flat land aridity of the material world, the more we support and promote life.

Life loves a crazy genius more than a classic law abiding citizen who is intimidated by objective facts.

And that is my privilege as a self-conscious individual and source of all values. By defying the objective world I announce my life. By submitting to the objective world I pronounce my death. This does not mean that you are asked to jump from the fifth story of a high-rise building and try to defy gravity. On the contrary it means to push a spacecraft into outer space by overcoming the law of gravity.

■ In which world do we really live, the scientific, social, personal or subjective?

You are once again betraying reductionism and ignoring the holistic fact of life. Is there a way you can separate in a laboratory the scientific from the social, cultural, biological, and subjective? I would say that all these are categories created by the mind.

Mind divides in an effort to refashion reality. That is the creative enterprise of human beings. They want to participate in the creation of realities. You cannot reduce the subjective to the objective or the objective to the subjective, nor can you reduce the cultural to the psychological, or the psychological to the social. They all have realities in their own realms. This does not mean that you should not try to engage in reductionism or scientific and logical categorisation of events and facts.

What gives meaning and life to all these is the human enterprise and project, which has to be integral.

■ The complexity of situations is sometimes so hard that there can be no way of responding to them. Let me bring to your attention something which has happened to my friend. His wife committed suicide (owing to her work tension) leaving behind three beautiful children. And recently he has found somebody whom he wishes to marry. In spite of having faced the uncertainty and cruelty of fate, why are we forced to commit the same mistakes and tread on the same risky paths?

The lesson that one learns from one's past life is not that one should fold up and retreat but that one should find ways and means of avoiding past mistakes. The recluse and the renunciant often betray symptoms of a 'once bitten twice shy' attitude, which means that they have not learnt from their past experiences, but that those experiences have become traumas locking their self expression.

Uncertainty is a fact of life.

The man whose wife committed suicide and betrayed his trust leaving three beautiful children should not learn the wrong lessons from that experience. I am not recommending that he should marry a second time nor do I think that second marriage is a mistake. What I think is that he should go ahead if he has a biological and social need. If he thinks that marriage will obstruct his individual growth he should not opt for marriage. What I would recommend is to keep a range of options. When we consider one, we should not foreclose other options.

Uncertainty is a fact of life. Past experience, bitter or sweet should not condition your interpretation of the present experience beyond a limit. Your suggestion that we bump into the same dangers again and again in spite of warnings given by life is to be looked at differently.

Life is always for experiment. And one who experiments with life gains more and more from life.

Life is always for experiment. And one who experiments with life gains more and more from life. I am not going to suggest what this person should do given the circumstances that you have described. That privilege is his and his alone. But we can persuade him to look at the issue from all standpoints and let a spontaneous decision arise.

■ What is the goal of human life, according to you?

I should say the goal of human life is 'to know who I am', 'what is my place in this universe', and 'how can I express myself freely integrating my environment', which I would call freedom. I think it is an ongoing dynamic enterprise and the ultimate answer will always be unknown.

■ If I am the spiritual self, where has the deep-rooted sorrow come from?

Sorrow is a fact of life and also an interpretation of fact.

Sorrow is a fact of life and also an interpretation of fact. What we think is sorrowful on second thought may not be so. When we contemplate upon life dispassionately there is no sorrow but only understanding. When we engage in various enterprises and projects there is anxiety, apprehension and sorrow. We must learn to move from activity to reflection and vice versa and finally make activity a reflective project that will remove the negative content from the experience of sorrow, and help sorrow and pain become the fuel of life.

■ Why are we not comfortable with pain, both physical and psychological, and why do we try to avoid them? We want to be happy and comfortable. Why is pain so unnatural and unwelcome? Am I posing a theoretical question?

Trying to avoid pain is an impulsive response. When I step on a burning cigarbutt I unconsciously lift my foot; if somebody comes up to me carrying a weapon with a murderous intent, I automatically run away from him; when I see a tiger in front of me I immediately climb up a nearby tree.

It is a fact of life rather than a theoretical proposition that people try to avoid pain. It also shows that people are more impulsive than reflective. A reflective person understands pain much better than an impulsive person. A reflective person incorporates the evolutionary force of pain for his personal growth. I think what is important is a movement from impulsiveness to reflectivity.

■ Will the evolution of human intelligence always be threatened by the impediment of his emotional attributes? May be if we do away with the emotional mind, we can be perfect like the physical systems and machines which deliver maximum work efficiency!

It is an absurd suggestion that on removing the emotions human beings will become perfect. You have added to the absurdity by citing the example of machines. The very insignia of life is emotions, desires, motives, intentions and purposes. Without these life will be death. A machine will not move by itself. What is probably necessary is to develop soft skill, and channelise emotions to cultivate our intentions so that the energy generated is used as an evolutionary force rather than a disruptive force.

I cannot imagine life without emotions. Logical thinking and so-called intelligence based upon analytical faculties are not the cutting edge of life. Emotions are the flaming tip of life. Logical thinking only ratifies the *status quo* whereas emotion is the emerging sprout of growth from the shell of *status quo*. I would anytime recommend passion over reason, if I have to make a choice. But passion and reason together make a happy couple.

■ Can there be an answer to the classical question, 'who am I'?

No.

An answer will be an insult to that question. There can be explorations with the help of that question. The question takes us to peak after peak. There is no destination as such. There is only the ecstasy of self-exploration and expression. It is not the end but the endlessness that is our end. The self is the infinite, all encompassing, ever dynamic and ever expressing reality.

■ Can my subjectivity thrive without being in an inter-subjective world?

No. Your subjectivity is intricately interwoven with the inter-subjective and objective worlds. Your subjectivity is both the flower and seed of the world. It is the distanceless distance between the seed and the flower that makes the inter-subjective and objective universes appear. They are part of the mystery of the flower being the seed, and the seed being the flower and yet having a distance in between.

■ What is the primary goal and purpose of human life according to you?

That question is very primitive in the background of this evening's dialogue. I myself do not know what is the purpose of my life. I may say it is freedom or fulfillment of my total potentialities, or god consciousness, or embracing the world with my love, or becoming an all-knowing, all-powerful god myself, or becoming the subject incorporating the whole cosmos.

Your question involves two issues. What should be the goal of human beings and what is going to be the destiny of the human species. I can only say that this will be decided by the collective consciousness of free choice-making individuals. Whatever destination I reach as a natural process of evolution has to be the best prospect for the human species.

- Why are human relationships so tender, fragile and vulnerable, and, why do they often break down?

Does man choose his relationship or does he just find himself in a set of relationships? What is the binding force in relationships? Man is said to be a gregarious animal. I find relationships grow when all parties involved gain from the association. When the relationship tilts in favour of one against the other what holds the relationship is only the fear of loss, or uncertainties. If the purpose of relationship is mutual gain, then naturally the relationship will be dissolved when that purpose is not fulfilled on a sustainable level.

I think human beings come together due to biological, geographical, productive, or historical causes. Such associations have certain inbuilt advantages. To the extent they are advantageous the relationship will be smooth and lasting. When they are disadvantageous, the relationship becomes stormy and starts deteriorating.

I feel relationships also dissolve or dry up when the purpose is fulfilled, or when the purpose has no chance of being fulfilled. For example, the relationship between parents and children, husband and wife, ruler and ruled. They all become loosened when the avowed purposes are not fulfilled or when their initial projects are fulfilled.

Individuals are basically interested in their own fulfillment. If that involves an initial sacrifice they do not mind. But if it means endless sacrifice with no light at the end of the tunnel that relationship becomes unilateral, exploitative and unproductive. For a successful relationship parties involved should challenge each other continuously and must learn to grow together. A martyr psychology will not help to create fulfilling and sustained relationships. When an individual knows exactly what he wants from a relationship, and he is ready to share his intentions, then alone communication is possible, and he/she is able to organise the relationship on a mutually rewarding basis.

I am not a votary of lifelong relationships based on insecurities, fears, dominations and non-reciprocal sacrifices.

I am not a votary of lifelong relationships based on insecurities, fears, dominations and non-reciprocal sacrifices. I believe in give and take relationships. I believe in nourishing and cherishing relationships. It is the sustainability and the sense of wellbeing that a relationship generates which are more important. There is no harm in dissolving a relationship when it has outlived its purpose.

■ Does not relationship have a sacredness to it which is not measured by its teleological value but by its sheer existence?

The sacredness of a relationship cannot be quantified and institutionalised or brought into the framework of strict rules and regulations. A relationship cannot be sacred when one party becomes an object of exploitation and the other the beneficiary of that exploitation. Sacrifice has to be mutual. I believe that a sustainable relationship need not involve sacrifices detrimental to the sacrificed. I am not talking in terms of material rewards. I am talking in terms of energies and inspirations that motivate individuals to give and nourish a relationship. If both the parties are not self-motivated and inspired, the quality of that relationship suffers. I am not saying that sacrifice is not necessary in relationship but it has to be mutual, complementary and not destructive and slavish.

■ So, are forming of relationships and engaging in them finally driven by selfish motives and one-sided judgments about the quality of the relationship?

All relationships are self-seeking, self-exploring and self-expressing enterprises. Individuals in a relationship must reserve their rights and abilities to judge the motive of the other with the full knowledge that the other also has the same right to judge the validity and purity of the counterpart's motives.

All relationships are self-seeking, self-exploring and self-expressing enterprises.

Individuals are the source of values. The ultimate judge of value is the individual's satisfaction. If we snuff out the individuality in a relationship what we get would be an exploitative relationship that ceases to be challenging and which will lead to the ultimate death and collapse of both the individuals.

■ Let us take a situation of a couple who mutually challenge their intellectual and social capabilities and bring out the best in each other. If it so happens that one of them, due to disease or unforeseen reasons becomes physically crippled and is unable to exercise intellectual and social capabilities will the other renounce her/him since she/he will be no longer provocative and challenging enough to bring out the other's potential?

I think – that a self-respecting individual will develop enough resources to handle his/her personal and public crises independently. By some chance if he becomes incapable there is enough compassion in this world that will manifest through his/her partner.

When I say 'growing together' it is not only in terms of financial resources or social influences, it also means ethical and moral perspectives, love, compassion and responsibilities. I would consider him a brute who abandons his friend when he/she is lying helpless because of injury, or illness or old age.

The best of human emotions come out when an individual is challenged in this manner. A person who ruthlessly abandons a friend in need, or, in danger, is not the picture of the individual that I have in mind.

6

Death and Existence

■ Can we have a working definition of death and existence?

Would you like to define death and existence in your own words?

■ I would like to think, at least conceptually, that death is the termination of my physical existence, and existence means the larger term which would relate to many different kinds of individuated and subjective experiences. Because, both death and existence, though the latter connotes a larger term, refer to limited thinking in the context of time–space and causal events. The moment we talk about death or existence, the immediate conceivable question will be 'whose'. Therefore a limited reference is unavoidable for both 'death' and 'existence' if I have to conceptualise these phenomena.

I would like to juxtapose death with life rather than existence. Death could mean the change of form, structure, location and function of a given phenomenon. Life in the natural sense is understood as the ability to receive and respond to stimulus, to reproduce, to have a minimum set of survival instincts to encounter hostile or friendly environment.

Death could mean the change of form, structure, location and function of a given phenomenon.

One could conceive of life existing in different forms without extinction with a certain continuity of memory. For example: when a tree dies or disintegrates it will continue to exist in various other life forms as seeds and saplings, fungi, bacteria etc. One can see some kind of a continuity even in inert matter like minerals and stones.

It is very difficult to distinguish between life and death except that they are two ways in which existence manifests. You can say that in the spectrum of existence at one end you can see life, and at the other end you can see death in its absolute sense. Otherwise their fault-lines look diffused; an apparently dead body actually seethes with life forms.

However, the context in which we discuss death and life is something different. We are talking about the clinical death of a complex organism where the functions of the organs stop and the organism cease to exist as a unity.

As human beings, when we contemplate upon death, our concern is further narrowed when we think of a human being who is no more available for interactions and participation in the social discourse. At another end, scientists are thinking of creating a living and self-perpetuating organism, however simple it may be, from nonliving matter. Theoretically this may be possible since living tissues and cells are made of molecules combined from nonliving atoms. The modern medical world is increasingly coming to a position where transplants and artificial implants can replace almost all organs of the human body. Medical science has proved that even if 75 per cent of the non-critical part of the brain is removed a human being can function in a more or less normal fashion.

From all this, the question which arises about life and death is essentially human-centred and moralistic, rather than life-centred and scientific. Devoid of human emotions involved and related ethical issues, death loses much of its significance. Life seems to be more prevalent, and death only a change of life form. Still death raises ethical, existential and scientific questions.

The question about death is basically centred on 'who is dying' than 'what is death'. Is death extinction or disintegration of an entity? Or is it only a change of frame of reference, or a change of location of that entity? Meaning, is there anything enduring and indivisible which death cannot touch? For whom does death happen and for whom is death an experience of change? Death also refers to the end of the continuity of memory. The question 'What is death' is intimately related to the question of an enduring and indivisible subject.

The question about death is basically centred on 'who is dying' than 'what is death'.

The wisdom tradition that I belong to believes that the disintegration of a complex organism like the human brain and the nervous system is not the end of the mind that operates the brain and nervous system. The history of the mind with its accumulated memory survives the disintegration of the organism. When the mind reestablishes its connection with the self through the process of awakening or deepening understanding, it ends its isolationist pursuits and becomes an instrument of infinite intelligence. This state is called the death of the mind or the birth of the spirit.

I do not want to get into that area of discussion at this point. From the body-mind-soul perspective death is only a change and not extinction, and it has meaning only with reference to a changeless subject.

■ Life is meaningful between the extent of birth and death. Why do you think we are so enslaved and restricted to the period in between, controlled by physical death?

I have already expressed my thoughts on the meaning of life and death. When we discuss these two ideas in the context of the human being, it is mixed with feelings, memories and judgments all centred on the subject.

I do not see the body as a constraining or confining object. I look upon the body as an instrument for self-unfoldment.

To me, disintegration of one body, what we call as physical death, is quite natural and advantageous, like the wearing out of a car, or dilapidation of a building. It gives an opportunity to buy a new car, or to build a new house according to my changed needs and aesthetics. Still the fact remains that the extinction of the physical body comes as a final and absolute event.

There is no way one can recall memories of one's experience in a previous body. Memory is an important component of identity. At the same time I can think of an identity beyond memory. I can also envisage a self that can operate out of spontaneity unconditioned at least by psychological memories. When I say psychological memories it is only to distinguish *between* memories of facts and factual experiences. Until I have a way of recalling my memories of past lives, I have no means of believing that I can survive physical death.

On one side, I have the firm faith that my essential nature is the spirit, and that mind and brain are only transient phenomena, and that physical death is only an experience and not my extinction. On the other side, I have no way of remembering the fact that I survived several physical bodies.

I have evidence for the existence of the spirit in the sense the invocation of the spirit in thoughts and deeds is possible and as a general sense of wellness. I think we have a lot of work to do in this area to bridge the gap between our beliefs and rational understanding. I have no clear answer to what happens to the individual after death. But I have no hesitation in saying that physical death is not the end of the individual. I am ready to stake physical death for ideas closer to my heart.

■ However much we philosophise the 'body' is a hard reality to ignore. Why is it that we have no other existence other than the physical existence where we share a common world, participate and exchange ideas, though we are aware of our mental and spiritual realms of existence? Why is physical existence and physical reality so real?

It depends upon your definition of reality. If reality means that which does not change in time, the body is not real. The body does change and disappear over time. If reality means that which is experienced, then the body is real because it is the most intimate experience. If reality means that you have no identity other than body then it is an area of dispute.

I am one who believes that I have an identity other than the body. It makes me fearless. It gives me a sense of deeper identity. It gives me the ability to discipline the body. It helps me to look at the body as an instrument of experience rather than the very subject of experience.

I am one who believes that I have an identity other than the body. It makes me fearless.

There is something deeper and more profound that I am privy to than the ordinary functions of the body – functions like receiving and responding to stimuli, eating, replicating, becoming old etc. I am something more than what is normally understood as the body. Some people believe that we do not actualise the full potential of the brain nor do we allow the body to bring out its full powers. In other words, the brain has access to infinite reservoirs of energy and intelligence.

All these ideas are involved when I say that I am not the body and I do not cease to exist when the body disintegrates. But it does not mean that after the death of the body I might 'float' like a ghost or phantom as we hear in popular superstitious beliefs and stories.

■ I get confused when I think that all that I do, create, understand, share and participate in has a meaning only as long as my bodily existence and my experience of the world remain intact. What is the purpose of knowledge and experience which I cannot carry forth, to probably other worlds, after my physical death?

I fully share your anxiety and concern regarding your inability to store your experiences and knowledge beyond the body and the brain. I should be able to drive a car on the roads in another city even if I leave behind my car in my home city. Because my knowledge of driving is distinct from the car without which of course I cannot drive. But do I have any purpose in acquiring knowledge and experience other than maintaining this body? Will I be able to maintain this body with the knowledge and experience available to me? Does not the maintenance of the body require far more knowledge and experience than I have acquired in one lifetime? In that sense, nature has enough intelligence to maintain life and living bodies in her own unique ways. In her scheme of things memory and knowledge are maintained in an unbroken chain at the genetic level or the subatomic level. Our need for preserving historical and cultural identities seems to require human effort; that will be the project for modern studies in consciousness.

I think that the question of death is essentially a question of retaining cultural memories, memories of tribal and social lives.

I think that the question of death is essentially a question of retaining cultural memories, memories of tribal and social lives. When I think about death, I think about the death of a father or a son, a wife a husband, a scholar or a saint, not the death of a spirit or a mind or an atom or a gene. I think that actually we have to define what is death and whose death is really perturbing.

■ I know that I am more than my body. I also know that even that knowledge (that I am more than my body) is expressed and therefore limited by my physical existence. What do you think of the possibility of having a medium (body or any other) which is not controlled by birth and death and therefore by time–space and causal events?

I strongly believe in such a dimension for the individual. It could be my imagination also. But one cannot imagine something that is not possible in some way or the other in this universe. At the same time I do not think that the evidence is ubiquitous to scientifically prove the existence of a disembodied state for the individual. It is rumoured that otherwise intelligent, creative and successful citizens were sometimes able to talk to their dead wives or sons or close friends through some medium. I strongly suspect that all these experiences belong to the realm of imagination without any corresponding reality.

To me immortality is fearless and timeless spontaneity.

To me immortality is fearless and timeless spontaneity. Immortality is not contingent upon the physical body. Immortality of brain, I do not know, whether immortality of the brain is a desirable state or not. I leave that question to the physical scientists.

- Can I have a body without the mind facilitating my thoughts? Can I have a mind without the body facilitating its expression? Can I have a spirit which transcends both and still bears an identity with reference to my individuality, defined by my own body and mind?

I think that all these states are possible. The body, mind and spirit have their own realities and existence. Thoughts can exist without the body. Body can exist without thoughts. And spirit can exist without both. People are able to think of machines and zombies that work without thoughts, and thoughts without manifestation through the body. A thought, which is a mere idea, does not affect any feelings or initiate any activity. The spirit, which is still deeper, is the field of all potentialities. In our normal experiences these three – body, mind and spirit – function interdependently.

Grief involved in death is purely cultural and psychological, which can be overcome by philosophical reflection.

- Why is death so painful and birth relatively a happy event?

Sorrow and grief that we go through at the death of near and dear ones is due to a sense of loss, of something which we possess and depend on for financial or emotional security. Grief involved in death is purely cultural and psychological, which can be overcome by philosophical reflection.

What is more intellectually challenging about death is our inability to rectify it and bring life back to *status quo ante.* Psychological grief can be the subject of poetic reflection and exuberance, not a subject of serious intellectual investigation. When Buddha was requested by the grieving mother to bring her dead son back to life, he quietly asked her to get a handful of sesame seeds from any house that was not struck by the sword of death. I do not think that death is such a painful experience. It is only an intellectual challenge.

■ How can I cope with the death of my loved ones?

Nobody would like to see the death of his/her loved ones. But the truth is that nobody loves anybody but for themselves. I love my children because they make me happy.

The truth is that nobody loves anybody but for themselves.

That means ultimately I love myself. So too, through philosophical reflection, one can come to the realisation that my inconsolable grief is due to my own insecurity, and that can be overcome only by developing a vision of life based on facts and the perception of my potentialities.

Once I know that those born shall die and I have to face my insecurity on my own, then my dependence on others ends relatively and, to that extent, I am able to cope with the death of my near and dear ones.

■ Animals hardly mourn death. Is our fear and grief about death a cultural offshoot?

Absolutely! It is the cultural institution, bonds and mutual investments we make, and, expectations that we have, which is the main cause for grief. There can be stray incidents where animals like elephants and dogs or birds like the crow show some kind of empathy for their dead. Recently I heard that a he-elephant died fasting on the spot where his beloved she-elephant died a month earlier. We do not know the reason for such uncommon behaviour. But humans grieve more than animals. Grief is essentially a cultural phenomenon.

■ The uncertainty about death is universal beyond gender, age and identity. Still it is common that the fear of death looms larger as one grows older. Could you suggest how the elderly harbour fear/rampant thoughts about death, and the relatively younger ones have a mature understanding and approach towards it?

Since fear of death is basically a cultural phenomenon, every culture has devised methods and ways to cope with the inevitable death that occurs due to old age, accident, illness or congenital defects. These methods are rituals; philosophical understanding or surrender to the will of God who has the ultimate say in such matters, alone help.

Any cultured person as he grows old prepares himself for death, accepting it as the natural and logical end of physical life. People do not have to die by accident or illness provided they lead a righteous and alert life. Congenital defects bring their own intelligence and life manages the situation satisfactorily. It is the relatives of those people who suffer more than the victim. That is again a cultural trait that has to be overcome by philosophical understanding or social healing. This is how societies cope with the inevitable prospect of the death of its members.

■ It seems we have created a complex web of relationships, fear, insecurity, identity crises and the inevitable agony about death – all the products of our cultural and social behaviour. Has culture restricted our experience and intelligence?

Yes and no! All these emotional traits that you describe are the expressions of a complex organism actively interacting and growing in a social structure. We are afraid of death since we have invested, created, and accumulated so much. Anxieties and insecurities are all a result of acquisition and attachment. One who has nothing has the least fear of loss and death. He would instinctively try to run away from danger when he meets with a threat to his life, but when he meets with death he would just die.

Metaphorical thinking, cultural and historical memories, and imagination are other reasons for the fear of death. The bottom line is, 'I am not afraid of death except that it reminds me of my own death'. Your own death is something that you have no clue about. Hence you live in fear.

■ Is death the primary reason for the fear and insecurity which runs in and through human life?

The main reason for insecurity and fear is apprehension of loss. Death is the final loss. It takes away everything with it. Death is a cumulative phenomenon and not just the leaving of the last breath.

■ What is your view on transmigration, rebirth and para-psychological experiences?

I would like to believe in the possibility of rebirth, transmigration and para-psychological experiences. It is every individual's dream to have an identity beyond the perishable body in order to carry forward the memories of the past into the future, and to have an enduring identity. It is also our desire to expand the scope of our senses and our mind and access information from fields inaccessible to us through our limited sense organs. Science and technology to a large extent are doing it for us. We are able to penetrate into the dark regions of existence with the help of advances in technologies and brain research.

The wisdom tradition that I belong to upholds the view that the individual has a mind and spirit which survive his physical death and which gain new physical bodies to have fresh experiences according to his/her knowledge and the deeds in his/her previous birth. This contention seems very reasonable to me, because it is knowledge and knowledge-based activity that determines the individual's experience in his/her current life. Therefore they must influence his/her experiences in future lives as well.

According to the *Gītā* death is no more than a change of garments. The future of the psychic individual is determined by the last thought before life leaves the body. The quality, depth and direction of thoughts determine the destiny of the psychic self after leaving the physical body.

I tend to believe in all these insights and would like to organise my life according to these insights rather than just eating, reproducing, and waiting melancholically for the final disintegration of the physical body. But I will apply this principle rationally and practically and will not allow myself to live in a dreamland of my private fantasies. I would always like to incorporate modern scientific views and discoveries into the realisation of my desire to be immortal.

■ Do you think mankind has learned enough from the phenomenon of death?

Mankind has not learned anything from the phenomenon of death. He has not become humble nor has he become detached. He has not learned to leave the physical world happily or to leave a happy world behind him.

Mankind has not learned anything from the phenomenon of death. He has not become humble nor has he become detached.

Philosophers have no clue about death. Scientists are making much noise and conducting bold experiments to understand the phenomenon of death and the process of dying, and to retrieve human consciousness, subjectivity and memory from the bottomless dark pit of death.

I think that the next century will witness considerable strides in understanding death and realising our cherished goal of immortality.

■ When I reflect on the strong sense of myself, which I have all through me expressed through my body, I also 'feel' that 'I' cannot be extinguished by the disappearance of my body. But the urge to express in and through it is so strong that I cannot imagine what I will do when my body will no more be available for me one fine morning!

To me, body is a series of information, and is a modification of eternal consciousness that is my real identity. Hence the end of one body is not my end or my expressions. The body need not be gross and heavy with physical extensions. It can be very subtle and still be expressing my intentions and energies.

I do agree with you that there should be a mechanism for self-expression. Just as the computer chips are becoming smaller and smaller while containing more and more information, the body can be subtler and smaller. I look forward to a situation, of which the *Yogic* seers speak, the possibility of compressing the mass of the body and expanding it at will, which will be a great leap in evolution.

We have to have unconventional reflections and ideas on the nature and function of the body, which will be another area for scientific interest and investigation.

■ Death is an important aspect in almost all *Tāntric* literature, be it Hindu, Jain or Buddhist. Could you please reflect?

Tantra is practiced in Hinduism, Jainism and Buddhism by a considerable number of devotees, though it is not the mainstream religion in any of these traditions.

Tantra worships death as the ultimate reality and sex as life. Death is the ultimate form of sex. Life is ephemeral. Death is permanent, unalterable and final. Life is a flicker. Death is the fixed centre of existence.

Tāntrics take the burial ground as the symbol of death, where life comes to rest after its temporary sojourn. *Tantra* worships the dead body. *Tāntrics* cook their meal in the funeral pyre. They mix all ingredients and cook it in a skull. *Tantra* also envisions a reality that is composed of opposites and contradictions. It sees death and life, filth and perfume, lust and love, cruelty and compassion, poison and nectar as aspects of the same reality. Nothing is repugnant to *Tāntrics*. Nor is anything dear to them.

I think *Tantra* is a neurotic reaction to the puzzle of life. It looks grand from a distance. But when it is practised it is vulgar, insensitive, abhorrent and devoid of any aesthetic sensibility. Sometimes I feel that the *Tāntric* is one who possesses all but displaces everything. It is like hair that instead of being on one's head falls into food. You may ask how does it matter. Theoretically a correct poser but aesthetically incorrect!

The only *Tāntric* principle which is accepted by the mainstream spirituality is that however base an energy, it can be raised through a process of discipline and purification. The raw energy can be brought to a state of purity and perfection. Poison can be turned into nectar. Lust can be turned into love. Wrath can be turned into compassion. Matter can metamorphose into spirit. Man can become God. *Tantra* takes nothing as irretrievably lost. In that sense, a *Tāntric* is like an artist who picks up abandoned material and makes a piece of art.

We cannot wholly give up the tradition of *Tantra* simply because of the aberrations, vulgarities and baseness that have crept into its practice. If the practitioner of *Tantra* has integrity, then *Tantra* can become a powerful tool for global integration, self-transformation and spiritual realisation.

■ Why do human interactions and institutions develop as if death is not even a remote possibility? Why are we not able to make it an important factor in the way we create institutions and conduct social exchanges?

Whether we recognise it or not, every human institution follows the same pattern of birth, growth, decay and death; be it a country, political system, family or religion. Civilisations have appeared and disappeared. Nations that have existed for long periods of time have been wiped out. Ideas like communism, religious practices like human sacrifice, institutions like the League of Nations, empires like the Roman and British have all died and disappeared. Just as individual human beings work, fight, and hoard as though they are going to live permanently on this planet, societies create institutions and consider that those institutions will remain forever. This is human folly. May be this folly is the secret of man's hope that somehow or the other, in spite of the mad dance of death, he will be the ultimate victor and will proclaim the immortality of his spirit.

Whether we recognise it or not, every human institution follows the same pattern of birth, growth, decay and death.

■ Why is it that I do not have a choice of the body into which I shall be born in my next life?

Theoretically, the body that you are born in was ordered by you, and was manufactured as per your instructions and delivered on your command. But when the body is delivered you change your mind like any shopper who shows keen interest in a product till he buys it. When the package reaches his home he loses interest and looks for some other product.

I also find it difficult to believe that we do not like our bodies. In fact we are all madly in love with our bodies. It is an ambivalent relationship of hate and love. Maybe you also have a desire to embrace all bodies, to communicate and access the information and intelligence available in all bodies so that you can realise the potential of being a cosmic person.

- Are birth and death inevitable? If birth and death are not there will there still be existence, and individuated lives extended by some other kind of time-space and causal structures?

I think that birth and death, which means constant change, are of the nature of phenomena. Reality is so dynamic that it is not the same at any given moment. It is infinitely creative and spontaneous.

It is not the change, that is the birth or the death of an instrument or a body, which provokes a question like yours. It is the confusion regarding the subject 'I'. It is the anxiety of the apparent loss of 'I' when the physical body dies which provokes the question about the significance of birth and death. Just as a body exists in this framework of time and space and in a causal relationship there can be another framework made up of some other components to which the self or 'I' can relate. At this moment these are all in the realm of speculation and probabilities. I strongly believe that such dimensions of existence are possible.

- The famous verse in the *Bhagavad Gītā* suggests two different ideas about death and existence. In one context it says that just as we throw away old clothes, when the time comes we throw away our old bodies and get new ones. In another context it says that there is no non-existence for existence, and that the non-existent can never exist. How should one understand existence in these two contexts?

The *Bhagavad Gītā* like any other scripture is ambivalent on the nature of immortality. Is it the immortality of a universal spirit or the individuated soul that is distinct from the mind–body complex? The illustration of equating the body with a draped garment around the soul, which is cast off when the garment has become torn and tattered suggests that the soul is a limited and individuated entity. The description that the soul is never born nor ever dies, nor does it become and un-become, does not suit this limited perception of the soul and the idea that the soul moves from body to body, travelling through a very subtle and invisible corridor of time and space.

There are religions, like the Semitic, that do not believe in the transmigrating soul. They believe that there is only one creation with a beginning and an end, and that there is only one birth for the soul. Those who believe in a limited soul themselves are divided into these two conceptions of the soul: a transmigrating soul and a once born soul. The *Gītā* and the other Eastern traditions talk also about a universal soul, and that the immortality of the soul is attained when the individual soul merges with the universal soul. The *Advaita* tradition talks about an eternal, all-pervading, immortal, non-transmigrating *Ātman* that is the true nature of the soul or the spirit.

I find that there are many ambiguities in these standpoints. But all of them point to the fact that man's destiny is to become the immortal, intelligent, self-conscious spirit.

■ In *Vedāntic* literature, existence, consciousness and bliss are said to be the nature of the highest reality. Do the three connote the same kind of 'existence'?

Yes, all the three denote the same existence. Existence is consciousness. Consciousness is bliss. And existence-consciousness-bliss is infinite. That is *śiva*, goodness. That is *sundaram*, beautiful. These are not the adjectives of a noun, or the qualities of a substance. They are the same and identical through and through. Ultimately it is said that this is the nature of the subject, the 'I'. To sum up *sat=cit, cit=ānanda, ānanda=śiva, śiva=sundaram, sundaram=I*, the first person pronoun which is self-evident and the invariable experience of you and I.

■ What is the significance of post-death religious rituals in the name of the deceased? Is there something more than the cultural responses to death?

There must be some correlation between the needs of the dead and the deeds of the living that express as these rituals.

I would not reduce the post-death rituals to merely cultural and psychological coping processes though they are heavily influenced by the culture and psychology of the group that performs these rituals. There must be some correlation between the needs of the dead and the deeds of the living that express as these rituals.

Every ritual produces unique vibrations and

energies which not only helps the survivors of the deceased to cope with the loss – both physical and subtle – but also help the dead to find their way in the post-mortem journey. To my thinking, rituals influence deeper layers of energies and hence they become important in our striving towards immortality and the discovery of a deeper existence than the merely physical.

■ For whom is life/existence worse and more sorrowful? For the dead one or for the loved ones of the dead?

For the living who survive the dead! On second thought, I feel even the dead person who has memories of associations of good and bad experiences might be feeling bad for leaving behind a known set of circumstances.

From the standpoint of practical experience I find that the one who is left behind feels more sadness and grief than the one who embarks on a long journey. Therefore the dead feel less sorrowful than the living.

■ What kind of life is/will be more rewarding and joyful: physical life extended between birth and death, or spiritual existence which adheres on the self which transcends birth and death?

I would not compartmentalise life into physical, mental and spiritual. All the three are of the same source and influence one another and act in unison. One cannot exist without the other since they are not separate from one another.

The idea of a life free from the limiting conditions of time–

space and body, free from the chores of eating, growing, excreting and dying is merely speculative. One has to discover one's freedom. Freedom of the spirit is in spite of the body. The body does not limit the freedom of the spirit. A bird's flight, though conditioned, is not determined by the wingspan and the direction of its tail. They are only enhancing factors. The body is a tool for self-expression, and the spirit makes and unmakes bodies, and hence is never determined by this tool.

■ Life is based on creative expressions. To live is to create, whether it is physical, intellectual or spiritual creativity. But then creativity has a value which is bestowed on it by a life which is extended by birth and death, and causal events. Is not creativity also limited however profound it is? Knowledge, literature, science, art and for that matter any understanding and experience are ultimately to be regarded as the limited expressions of a limited existence.

A product cannot be limitless. It has to perish.

Creativity is not limited but creation is limited. Creativity is infinite and unending. But any complete product, or any specific creation, has to be limited. These two aspects of creativity, that its product is limited but resources are unlimited and the tools it uses are infinitely variegated, are not contradictory but complementary phenomena.

A product cannot be limitless. It has to perish. A limitless product has to have limitless processes. A limitless process cannot create a product. The very nature of creativity is that it creates products that are limited by a beginning and an end, birth and death. Birth and death are expressions of the infinite creativity of the spirit.

■ If we can somehow reorient causality and thereby form associations and correlations between experiences, events and objects separated by time and space, will we be able to lead a different life, may be one not initiated by birth and terminated by death?

Of course! That is what modern scientists are talking about– going back in time. If you can control time and its forward and backward movements, then death and life will mean a different experience to the subject. So too, memories will be no more of the past. They will also be of the future. It will be a state of complete fluidity and spontaneity. I am looking forward to such a situation where time and space are no more linear, as they are generally experienced.

Birth and death are expressions of the infinite creativity of the spirit.

■ Is physical existence prior or time-space? Each seems to be restricting the other and is responsible for the other's limited functions and expressions. With the instrumentality of my physical body and its attributes I can experience only causal events in time-space. The world of time-space and causal events can only have interactions with physical existence extended by time and space!

I think that time-space and physical bodies arise simultaneously. That is why you encounter these interactive and interdependent complexities in the experience of body and time-space. You cannot experience the body outside the context of time-space and you cannot experience time-space without the instrumentality of the physical body.

There might be ideas, pure thoughts, and mathematical expressions that do not have to exist in time–space though they apparently do not exist without the body.

It is a very complex situation, like the proverbial snake that swallows its own tail, depending upon the frame of reference and point of view we adopt. One becomes dependent on the other and as the point of view changes the reverse happens. There is a beautiful phrase in Sanskrit – 'the eaten eating the eater' (*adyate atti ca bhūtāni*). I think that this phrase summarises the kind of relationship that exists between time-space, causal events and the physical body. Śankarācārya calls this state as of 'indescribable correlations' (*anirvacaniya*) since the components that constitute reality constantly change place and relationship. The only way to live in this mad world is to become mad oneself.

7

Vedānta and Self-Knowledge

■ What is *Vedānta*?

Etymologically *Vedānta* means the end of the *Vedas*, that is, the culminating teaching of the *Vedic Ṛṣis*. It can also mean ultimate knowledge which is not historical and incremental, but which is revelatory and wholesome, dealing with ultimate reality. In another sense, you can say that *Vedānta* means self-knowledge, *adhyātmavidya*. Self is the enduring reality in all experiences, and is not influenced by experiences. Knowledge of the self cannot change in time. Śankarācārya says that *Vedānta* is a means of knowing with reference to ultimate reality, where inference and sense organs fail.

Vedānta includes all the unity statements of the *Upaniṣads*. A unity statement is represented by the often quoted pronouncement '*tattvamasi*', 'thou art that', in the sixth chapter of the *Cāndogya Upaniṣad*. The statement 'thou art that' means that all the values man wants to realise are hidden in his/her own consciousness. Reaching a goal is invoking hidden potentialities, the ultimate goal of humankind being unconditional happiness, all-embracing love, infinite creativity or, in other words, to become God. It is a matter of reaching deep into oneself and actualising one's own potential, interacting with the kaleidoscopically changing world.

Vedānta puts man and his awareness at the centre of the universe, and his freedom as the ultimate value of all activity. If you liberally interpret the meaning of *Vedānta*, it could mean any knowledge system be it Eastern or Western, African or Islamic, psychology or new-age theories, quantum physics or consciousness studies, which makes the individual the source of all energies and enables him to see his self as the locus of infinite potentialities, that which frees him from all limitations and encourages him to reach his infinite potential.

Śankarācārya says that *Vedānta* expounds the unity of the limited individual consciousness and the limitless universal consciousness. The discovery of that unity is the ultimate blessing of *Vedānta*.

■ Is *Vedānta* more than a philosophy?

Yes! *Vedānta* is philosophy as well as revelatory knowledge. Its exposition is based on ontological, epistemological and psychological perspectives. It deals with the ultimate nature of reality. It deals with the means of knowing the reality. It deals with the value system, which facilitates the knowing process. It deals with human nature on the subtle, causal and collective levels. It also deals with rituals of creating unconventional ways of looking into the human

Vedānta is philosophy as well as revelatory knowledge.

condition. *Vedānta* is a comprehensive worldview and a way of life.

■ From your explanation what I understand is that *Vedānta* is essentially a perspective or a distinct way of understanding and living. In that case how can we still uphold the foundational texts as the *pramāṇa*, including Śankarācārya's texts?

Vedānta is a living science, which means it is based on the individual's living experiences. It does not call for faith in a revelatory book, nor an unquestioned adherence to its tenets. It demands personal and unalterable experiences. Its authority is not Śankarācārya or the *Upaniṣad*s. Its authority is one's own direct experience that should not be contradictory to experiences of similarly enlightened people and which does not fly in the face of practical and logical intelligence.

Vedānta is not a perspective. It is the perspective of perspectives. It is not a locked wisdom. Its source is the individual enquirer and not the book. Its direction is one's own self and not towards the heavens. Its words come from the heart of the experiencer and not from the cold dead letters of the palm leaves. That is why I said earlier that any knowledge system, belonging to any place in the world and to any race, which reveals the integrity of the individual's subjective consciousness has to be called *Vedānta*.

In a very revealing passage, the *Upaniṣad* says that the subject consciousness is free from racial, religious, linguistic, cultural and historical conditioning. One who has gone to the depth of one's self will be an all-accommodating, tolerant, loving and engaging individual.

■ Any other philosophical school could make the claims you have made about *Vedānta*, that theirs is an all-encompassing perspective of perspectives.

The proselytising religions of the world which have their wisdom locked in their books and their interpreters, and who condemn man to the perspectives revealed in those books, and whose Gods and prophets claim a superior authority disallowing man to look into his soul, are sectarian and parochial and cannot claim to be a perspective of perspectives.

Any system that does not give the individual freedom, and respect his autonomous self, cannot be called *Vedāntic*. I would put that as the test for the claim made by any religion for universal acceptability and holistic perspective. Now it is for you, my friend, for yourself, by yourself, to test the claims made by any system of philosophy or theology.

■ I would like to keep philosophy and religion apart. I was particularly referring to other systems of Indian philosophy which also give importance to the freedom of the individual. Why *Vedānta* alone?

Nobody can give freedom to the individual unless the individual himself chooses to be free. That is precisely what *Vedānta* says. If any individual or system upholds that view it could be called *Vedāntic*.

■ In that case the whole of Indian philosophy could be considered as just one thought of *Vedānta*, rather than having the nine schools of thought!

I never disputed that there are differing views and systems of thought about man and his place in the universe and his destiny. I never said that all Indian systems of thought fall under the category of *Vedānta*. My contention is that any system of thought that accepts man and his subjective consciousness as the source of all values and helps him to tap those resources has to be called, generically, *Vedānta*. You may give any other name reflective of this idea.

■ Does not your view have a proselytising factor in it seeing the greatness of one system, and trying to include all other born, and yet to be born, philosophies under one big school of *Vedānta*?

My views will be proselytising if I force the other by threat or superior logical powers or by my charm to accept my views uncritically. If I engage the other in a dialogue and accept the other as the source of his values and me as the source of my values and whatever agreements we would have in the process without diminishing each other's uniqueness and freedom, I would not call that dialogue as proselytising.

Your question seems to have an underlying concern that a school of thought, devised by an individual or a culture imposing itself on another individual or culture, becomes exploitative and colonial. What I suggested was that all individuals should draw their values and energies from their own subjective consciousness and let a billion points of lights blink simultaneously.

■ What are the most important philosophical principles involved in *Vedānta*?

What are the philosophical principles you have in mind to measure *Vedānta* by?

■ I try to understand, as a philosopher, the distinct ways by which a specific system of thought has formed. Any philosophy would present distinct ideas or theories about god, nature of the world, means of knowledge and the nature of self. I would like to see whether *Vedānta* possesses the philosophical, or more specifically, the epistemological, metaphysical and eschatological components.

The statement in the *Bhagavad Gītā* – *ātmanā ātmānaṃ ātmani paśyan tuṣyati* – answers your questions. It says, by the self, seeing the self, in the self, one revels.

Vedānta reveals self as the metaphysical reality, self as the epistemological means, and self as the eschatological end of the individual. But to achieve this ultimate experience one has to prepare the mind by engaging in this world endowed with appropriate discipline and attitude. Since *Vedānta* is more interested in the experience of reality, its verbal structures, which I call metaphysical, are only temporary launching pads, and are like detachable rockets that burn down after performing their functions. *Vedānta* is a highly dynamic thought system, intrinsically opposed to rigid thought structures that become a hindrance to the realisation of truth.

■ How do we distinguish between *ātman* and *anātman*, self and non-self?

Ātman is your enduring subjective consciousness that is not negated by your experiences of the mental and material world.

The content of the experiencer is the *ātman*, and the content of the experience is the *anātman*. In another way, what is presented to consciousness is the non-self, what illumines the presentation is the self. The knower is the *ātman*, and the known is the *anātman*.

■ *Karma Siddhānta* explains the connection between unseen causes and seen results. It uses a rather circular logic to explain why certain things happen to certain people, or what decides the specificity of events for particular individuals.

Karma Siddhānta is a bold attempt to explain events, especially human experiences, in terms of the causation theory. Every event must have a cause or a set of causes. An event which is confined to the experience of a particular experiencer which he judges as good or bad, happy or unhappy has to be traced to the same experiencer, as the doer, or the intentor as its cause. Meaning, specific experiences must have specific causes just as a mango fruit which is a given object has a given and a specific cause in the mango seed.

It is the experiencer who interprets an event as good or bad. He himself must be the cause of the event in terms of good or bad actions.

It is the experiencer who interprets an event as good or bad.

Karma Siddhānta only upholds the view that every event must have a cause. It does not interpret the cause as good or bad, or the effect as good or bad. It is the experiencer who interprets this according to his or her value system.

■ I remember the talk once you gave on 'why bad things happen to good people'. Why is it that people who do comparatively good things suffer for no apparent reason in their present life? Or what decides that somebody is poor and another is rich? Or what decides the massive disappearance of a community of people through natural disasters?

That was only the first part of my lecture, 'Why bad things happen to good people'. The second part of my lecture dealt with 'What happens to good people when bad things happen to them'. I also interposed another question: 'Why good things happen to bad people'.

It all depends upon your definition of 'good', 'bad' and the 'individual'. It involves value judgments. I do not think being born in a poor family is a great calamity. Nor is it a great advantage to be born in a rich family. When all ultimately die, a large number of people dying due to natural calamities cannot be said good or bad.

I would like to bring a holistic perspective to these happenings. When I think dispassionately, I do not think my death will be a calamity, nor as something bad happening to me. If it is a question of avoiding calamities which causes suffering to a large number of people, and if it is a question of human incapacities or ignorance, I would say that we should work towards overcoming these deficiencies and defects and create conditions where such suffering could be reduced or eliminated.

Karma Siddhānta is, basically, a theory of moral causation that can be read backwards or forwards. Read backwards it says that when an individual interprets an experience as good or bad he assumes responsibility for what is happening to him. He is willing to take charge of his destiny by avoiding bad and courting good. In the process he gains a perspective wherein he becomes less judgmental and more tolerant. That is how I look at the *karma* theory and the understanding of 'good' and 'bad'.

■ Is there something called destiny? Is the fate of a person decided beforehand? For example: the painful event of a group of school children on a parade on that fateful morning of the earthquake in Kutch in 2000, and all died!

Why is there pain? What is the reason for so many inequalities and cruelties that we see around?

If you extrapolate private grief and universalise it these kind of shallow questions would arise in the mind. If you accept death as the flip side of life, school children dying in an earthquake is like any death happening anywhere to anybody.

I would put the question differently. Could we have avoided that tragedy? Could we have built better buildings? Could we have taken necessary precautions before marching these children through narrow lanes hemmed in by dilapidated buildings? It is more a question of human error, of callousness and casualness. If you ask wrong questions you will definitely get wrong answers.

Regarding the theory of destiny it is as good or bad as any other theory. The only question is how does it affect human behaviour. I have seen people believing in destiny, that man's fate is written by God in heaven, that everything is providential, that man has no initiative in drawing up his destiny, and what is happening to him is fated to happen. Some remarkably intelligent, agile and highly successful people believe in such ideas. A few others who have the same belief lead a docile, phlegmatic and resigned life.

I find that apart from these theories we uphold we have a basic intelligence with which we handle daily problems of life. I would like to understand that intelligence rather than the theories expounded on destiny and freewill.

- If experience (*anubhava*) and logic (*yukti*) are the twin factors for validating truth, how can I dismiss my experience of myself as a physical and psychological being, the experience of which is prior to any other experience?

If the present experience is negated by a later experience those sublatable experiences cannot be accepted as defining one's identity. They just remain as memories. One's identity cannot be reduced to mere memories. Your memories may colour your identity like a hibiscus colours the identity of a crystal. But the colour can never become the true identity of the crystal. Nor can the colour ever participate in determining the identity of the crystal.

You are not called upon to deny your physical and psychological being.

You are not called upon to deny your physical and psychological being. What you are called upon to do is to understand the nature of those experiences as something that is flexible and fleeting.

■ What is the borderline between eternal (*nitya*) and ephemeral (*anitya*), since experience in both cases is the primary factor?

The borderline is between the experiencer and the experienced. It is a very difficult line to draw since there is an incessant intercourse between the experiencer and the experienced. But one catches a glimpse of a thin line between the experiencer and the experienced or the eternal and the transient by bearing *sākṣibhāva* or non-judgmental witnesshood.

■ Is realistion of '*ahaṃ brahma asmi*' an occurrence for the *jiva* or the *ātman*? If it is for *jiva*, how can the limited have the knowledge of the unlimited? If it is for *ātman*, is there any need for the knowledge?

Realisation is not an event. It is the existent nature of *ātman. Jivatva* is only a proposition, a tool, to realise what is already there. Your question is like asking 'who wakes up from a dream, the waker or dreamer?', or 'who sees the dream, the waker or dreamer?'.

This is a classic example of conceptual categories of obfuscating actual understanding and leading to a paroxysm of baseless questions. *Jiva* has no reality. *Ātman* alone is real.

■ What is the meaning of self-ignorance and self-knowledge?

You use three words – ignorance, knowledge and meaning – all with reference to the 'self'. When you look at the issue what remains is only the self, free from knowledge, ignorance and meaning. These are all categories of an unseeing mind.

■ If ignorance and knowledge happen to the same self, they can recur at any time.

Let us not give reality to ignorance or knowledge. These are tools and devices used to bring in understanding, change cognitive processes and get a direct insight into the nature of reality. Categories of thought do not create the reality but only reveal the reality. In the realisation of that reality there is neither ignorance nor knowledge, whether in the past, present or future.

Let us not give reality to ignorance or knowledge.

■ How can the self be ignorant or knowledgeable about itself?

Nobody says that self is the subject having ignorance or the object of its own ignorance. The terms 'ignorance' and 'knowledge' are used to effect a cognitive change. They are not attributes of self. Therefore the question regarding the locus of ignorance betrays a lack of understanding of the epistemology of self-knowledge.

Ignorance is never accepted as an absolute category nor is knowledge. Both are modes of mind. The mode of ignorance is cancelled by the mode of knowledge that in turn gets self-cancelled in the revelation of the self. They are just words and thought modifications. They do not enjoy the status of unalterable truth.

■ Self-realisation is not an event in time. Dispassion, differentiation (*viveka*) and reflection (*vicāra*) lead to the knowledge of self. Are these events in time?

They are. They are all happenings in the brain. They are all self-cancelling processes. They do not perpetuate themselves when their goal is achieved. That is why Śankarācārya uses the word *mithya* and says that the problem as well as solution falls in the field of *mithya*. The 'teacher and disciple' and all such pairs fall in the field of *mithya*. It is a kind of vision that encompasses opposites, contradictions, and polarities and yet is not conditioned by them.

Śankarācārya in one context says that ignorance as a mode of *prakṛti* and knowledge as another mode of *prakṛti* do not affect the self. It is only the ignorant that identifies with *prakṛti* and her ever-changing modes. In another context, Śankarācārya says that the seeker has to control *tamas* and its dissipative and veiling energies with *rajas* and its goal-oriented dynamic energies, which, in turn, have to be controlled by *sattva* and its accommodating and balancing energies. And this in turn, has to be controlled by the spontaneity of the spirit which he calls 'transcendence'.

All these questions are polemical, and are based on rigid standpoints and *a priori* assumptions. But if you understand the spirit of *Vedāntic* propositions and its all-accommodating tolerance towards dissimilar systems many of these questions may not be posed and, if at all they are, posed only for clarification.

■ Though I may have different references to my self in terms of my age, my social roles and my own psychological states, I always have the sense of I-ness. But this I-ness is abstract and by itself has no meaning or depth. What is the benefit of having knowledge about the 'unchanging ontological self'?

Self-knowledge gives you greater understanding and control over your psychological, physical and environmental energies. It guards you from being limited by the body-mind conditions and helps you to become a master of those faculties. It gives you a moment-to-moment experience of transcendence, and freedom from the debilitating influence of the past. It gives you the ability to take charge of your life's destiny. It makes you approach life without the conditioning of the past but with the wisdom gained from the past.

You do not have a sense of the self in its deepest level. Nor can you reduce the self into categories of thought or modes of experiences. But the very suffocative nature of the body-mind and its ephemeral nature make you contemplative. In the depths of such contemplative crises one gets a sense of that which you describe as mere 'ontological I-ness'. I feel that without contact with that 'I-ness' and without inspiring and invoking its blessings, human life will be a melancholic parade of mental and material experiences.

- There are at least three ontological entities presented: *ātman*, *brahman* and *jiva*. What does the identity of *ātman* and *brahman* mean to *jiva*?

Ātman and *brahman* are *jiva* in its depth. As *jiva* deepens its identity, it touches *ātman* and then *brahman*. Essentially, they are the same. *Jiva,* the individuated conditioned consciousness, *ātman* the unconditioned pure consciousness and *brahman* the oceanic, unconditioned, pure consciousness are ontologically the same. Their ontological separateness is only a linguistic and logical convenience. It is like the relationship between a ripple, a wave and the ocean.

- To know that there is an abiding self on which are founded the variegated experiences, there seems to be no specific need for *Vedānta*. It is a matter of thinking or, may be, believing.

Thinking and believing can never take you to the abiding self. Abiding self is realised when you become the non-judgmental observer of thinking and believing. Then you find a relevance and meaning for all kinds of thinking and believing.

I do not say that the *Vedāntic* literature is an unavoidable component of self-enquiry. But it could be a valid and valuable guide. Ramaṇa Maharṣi proposes a method of direct enquiry aided by the question 'Who am I?' rather than the method of reflection, *vicāra*, on *Vedāntic* statements about unity or non-duality. The *Upaniṣads* themselves talk about relentless negation or uncompromising accommodation as paths.

Since *Vedānta* is not a system of belief to be accepted unquestionably and is only a guide that has to be intelligently followed by a seeker, the cynicism involved in the question has no relevance to the *Vedāntic* path. The concern of the questioner of being trapped in a parochial path is unfounded.

■ What is the place of *iśvara* in *Vedānta*?

Technically, *iśvara* is *brahman* engaged in the creative enterprise. *Brahman* expressing through *māya* manifests as the all-knowing and all-powerful *iśvara* who manifests as the whole universe. Since *māya* is the power of *brahman* to appear as the many without undergoing any fundamental change *iśvara*, *māya*, *jagat* (world) and *jiva* and the various instrumentalities of *jiva* like the five *kōṣās* all come under the category of *mithya* which is to be understood as *māya*.

In the *Vedāntic* system *iśvara* has a great role during the *sādhana* of the *sādhaka*. The *sādhaka* invokes *iśvara* as the guide and teacher. Together they dissolve into realisation. For an enlightened soul there is no *iśvara–jiva* duality. For him it is a dance of *jiva* and *iśvara*, like Kṛṣṇa dancing with Gopis in Vrindāvan on the banks of the Yamuna under a moonlit sky. *Brahman* is the ecstatic bliss such a union invokes.

- The understanding of the abiding self, *ātman* is at the level of causal thinking, that something changing needs something else which is changeless to exist. But the concept of *māya* is explained using more mystic characteristics than a realistic description. For example, in *Vivekacudāmoṇi* Śankarācārya says it is neither *sat* nor *asat*, different or similar, and cannot be described. So the experience of the world is explained to be as sublated by the removal of *māya* which happens in a trans-spatiotemporal state. So self-knowledge seems to be not basic attitudinal changes and a different worldview, but a magical, transcendental experience which has to happen!

Actually self-knowledge is all these steps put together. Logical thinking will lead you to the conviction that there is a changeless, invisible and indivisible substratum. Further understanding will take you to the conclusion that this substratum has to be subjective. At the same time you confront a consistent flow of experiences that is full of inexplicable contradictions defying logical categorisation. You find it difficult to draw the line between the real and the unreal, the invisible substratum and phenomenal world, subject and object.

Then, in order to read the book of life, you move from the realm of logic to the realm of psychic disciplines to fill the blanks that logic has left behind. It is during that period that you call forth psychic forces and various kinds of disciplines that involve imagination and a subtle use of denial and redirecting of the flow of psychic energy.

It is not just thinking. It is more related to the realm of passions and drives, feelings, unconscious, the nervous system etc. As a result the whole reality map changes and the so-called transcendental experience or a deepened understanding of ordinary experiences happen. The final realisation, which is a non-event, happens as a result of all this. Self-realisation is not just a logical conclusion, emotional turbulence, or a world denying experience. One has to go through it to experience its full blast.

- What is the experience of the world? Is it physical, social, and cultural or a creation of my own birth, which collapses into myself with my death?

When you say 'world collapsing into yourself at your death', I am sure you do not mean a total extinction of your own self. Or do you mean, your death is your extinction and the extinction of the world? Or do you mean both collapse into something deeper and fundamental? They all are corollary questions.

My answer is that the experience–experiencer duality requires an existing real substratum. I believe in the *satkāryavāda* of *Vedānta* that for anything to become an object of experience, it must have reality as its substratum. Something cannot arise from nothing. In that sense you, your sociocultural and material environment, and the experiences you harvest out of them and your interpretations of those experiences are all part of your realities, though they all change.

The experience–experiencer duality requires an existing real substratum.

What I believe is that there is a continuing identity that is intelligent and self-conscious in and through all these changing phenomena. Death is not the final end of the subjective consciousness. Death is only one among its experiences. In that understanding is the key to absolute knowledge.

Personally, I still play with the phenomenon of death with the tool provided by *Vedānta* with the full knowledge that I will die but with a question, 'Who is that dying I?' and, 'What happens to my spirit which never dies?'

- What is the difference/similarity between *avidya*, *māya* and *ajñāna*?

Ajñāna and *avidya* mean the same. It means exclusive understanding, seeing the tree and missing the forest, ignoring the background and focusing on the foreground. *Māya* is the general condition in which this tunnel vision occurs. When my knowledge becomes more inclusive, the veil lifts and the condition of *māya* instead of promoting my ignorance starts helping me to obtain deeper and deeper understanding. That which has been a hindrance becomes an enhancing factor. The lake that I was afraid of getting drowned in becomes a challenge, and an invitation for my aquatic skills, for me to plunge in and realise my potential to swim and play, to enjoy and celebrate.

- If I am the unborn and ever-existing, why am I born and why do I die? To conceive of my non-physical existence is to have beliefs or assumptions about something which is not available for concrete experience.

The very fact that all concrete experiences change and one wants to transcend transient experiences shows that there is a possibility of something enduring and immortal. My desire to be immortal is necessitated by transient experiences. The transcendent experience may not lend itself to be objectified. But it can be experienced as the source of all objective experiences. Transcendence can happen when transient experiences impinge upon one's awareness.

The very fact that all concrete experiences change and one wants to transcend transient experiences shows that there is a possibility of something enduring and immortal.

The experience of the transcendent, enduring reality is not concrete but it is something that is felt and understood in and through all experiences. I would call it a state of freedom from fear. A whole lot of our experiences, even about the empirical world for which we are ready to sacrifice ourselves, are not concrete; for example, the mother's love for the baby, the patriot's love for the nation, the lover's infatuation for the beloved. These are all very ethereal though it is possible to break down the emotions involved in these experiences into chemical constituents and neural processes.

■ What is *antahkaraṇaśuddhi* and how do I obtain it and benefit from it?

Antahkaraṇaśuddhi is non-reaction to environmental challenges. On the positive side, it is the appropriate response to situations, a response that is not corrupted by extreme likes and dislikes. As a result the mind becomes mature, the intellect gains clarity, and emotions become positive, which enables the individual to interact in synergy with the environment.

Every encounter becomes an inspiring challenge that helps the individual unleash his inner potentialities, which we call as god-realisation or *samadhi*. People from different cultures and belonging to different religions attain balance of mind by cultivating the appropriate attitudes. A Hindu will say '*Kṛṣṇārpaṇamastu*'– that is, 'All my actions and their fruits are an offering to Kṛṣṇa. A Muslim will say '*Inshallah*', that is, 'God's will.' A Christian will say '*Amen*', that is, 'So be it.' A nonbeliever will say that the uncertain consequences of risks are to be taken in one's stride.

■ What are the tools for self-realisation?

First, it is the understanding that subjective consciousness that is self-evident in all experiences is the source of all values like intelligence, health and happiness. Second, these values can be realised through interaction with the environment and progressive realisation of expansive and higher goals set in tune with one's talents and training. Third, a learning attitude to life and an empathic relationship with the world and the realisation that to exist is to coexist, and, to succeed is to help everybody to gain their own successes.

■ *Vedānta* talks about *pañcabhuta* to explain the external world; three bodies to explain waking, dream and deep sleep states; and *pañcakōśa* to explain the five levels of existence. Which 'I' should relate with which 'world'? Are we assuming multiple worlds and multiple existences?

These descriptions are approaches to the same phenomenon from different angles. *Pañcabhutās* are the basic building blocks of the five *kōśās* and the three states of mind. Consciousness expressing through the five *kōśās* and three states is the conditioned experiencer. You should not get confused by these various categorisations. They are different pointers to the same phenomenon.

■ If the knowledge of '*aham brahmāsmi*' is the key in *Vedānta* why do I have to meditate?

The knowledge that 'I am *Brahman*' will not come by mere thinking or by linguistic analysis of the sentence. *Brahman*-knowledge comes through detachment, meditation, silence, all-accommodating love, non-reaction and discipline on the physical and mental levels. Realisation happens instantaneously. But the ground has to be prepared elaborately and meticulously. Self-knowledge (*jñāna*) without discipline (*yoga)* is barren. And, discipline (*yoga*) without knowledge (*jñāna*) is a burden. Together it is an ecstatic dance all the way to the chamber of truth.

■ How do you see the personality of Ādi Śankarācārya?

Ādi Śankarācārya is one of the leading spiritual masters who secured Hinduism for India after a 1000-year period of predominance of Buddhism, and the social and moral decay caused by the misunderstanding of Buddhism as an atheistic and soulless religion. Śankarācārya integrated the best from Buddha's teachings and the *Vedic* traditions and revived Hinduism as a healthy river joined by different streams of ritualism, devotionalism and spiritual scholarship.

But Śankarācārya failed to create a sociopolitical and economic philosophy and appropriate institutions to galvanise the people into a productive and participative economic polity. This led to the overcoming of the Hindu society that showed strains of decadence and other-worldliness by the Islamic invaders.

The *varṇa-āśrama* system of dividing society and individual life into four quadrants, dividing workers into innumerable castes, and the whole dynamics based on birth and past *karma*/deeds–were left untouched by Śankarācārya. Ironically the spiritual insights he had, and the *Vedantic* philosophy he propounded, justified the re-organisation of society more equitably, alleviating people's suffering through rational human and institutional interventions.

If Śankarācārya is given the credit for solidifying Hinduism he must also take the blame for the slumber of Hindus under the Islamic and European rule for 1200 years.

If Śankarācārya is given the credit for solidifying Hinduism he must also take the blame for the slumber of Hindus under the Islamic and European rule for 1200 years. That is why I rate Veda Vyāsa higher than Śankarācārya and Buddha, though Vyāsa is more mythical than the historical personalities of Buddha and Śankarācārya. Vyāsa is a better and composite role model for the people and nation than the purely spiritual leadership offered by these two savants – Buddha and Śankarācārya. Still my heart goes to Śankarācārya for creating spiritual institutions by which he preserved the essential features of Hinduism and kept it secure from the invading marauders.

8

Guru-Śiṣya Tradition

■ A striking feature of the philosophical and spiritual traditions of the East is their foundation on the *Guru-Śiṣya parampara*. What exactly is the *Guru-Śiṣya* tradition and lineage?

Guru-Śiṣya tradition must have started because of the oral nature of the transference of knowledge from the teacher to the student. The person of the teacher was the repository of knowledge. There was no library or other means to store knowledge. The teacher did not have many instruments for teaching except his words and gestures.

The teacher is the most important functionary in the *Guru-Śiṣya* tradition. In ancient days skills, ethics, values and wisdom of the community was taught by the same person. Most often the teacher happened to be the father of the student. The student also had no other way to learn except by committing things to memory. He had to live in the proximity of the teacher, watch his behaviour and responses to various situations, and imbibe the teaching holistically.

Communities then were small. There was no change in the lifestyles of communities and hence memory oriented teaching and the teacher were the unquestioned and absolute authorities for learning skills, acquiring knowledge and values.

Another reason for the enduring quality of the *Guru-Śiṣya* tradition is the nature of Eastern spirituality. Spirituality is not a matter of faith and belief but of personal experience. Hence religion, spirituality and morality have to be taught by a teacher who had personal experience, commitment and practice. A teacher cannot be replaced by books or by any other mode of impersonal teaching.

Spirituality is not a matter of faith and belief but of personal experience.

There are three types of teachers in the Hindu tradition:

(i) *Upādhyāya,* who imparts knowledge of material sciences, that is, objective knowledge;

(ii) *Ācārya*, who imparts ethical and moral values which are more psychological and behavioural in nature; and

(iii) *Guru*, who imparts spiritual instructions.

Upādhyāya gives knowledge gained through objective scientific investigations. *Ācārya* imparts knowledge born of his own practices, the ethical knowledge of do-s and don't-s. The *Guru* imparts knowledge based on his personal realisation.

In the contemporary lingua, anybody who has authoritative knowledge born of long commitment and practice is called a *Guru*, like we have today, management *gurus*, sports *gurus*, and political *gurus*. Even in the modern educational system you have the – teacher-mentor for students, who acts as friend, guide, philosopher and confidante.

Guru-Śiṣya relationship is supposed to be the purest and the most ennobling and nourishing relationship. This tradition is the basis of culture, values and spirituality. In the *Cāṇdogya Upaniṣad* it is said, '*ācāryavān puruṣo veda*', which means, one who has a spiritual mentor alone comes to know the truth.

■ Was the *Guru-Śiṣya* tradition an inevitable need of the oral tradition then prevalent?

Yes! It was an inevitable need of the oral tradition. But I find that even in the modern educational system, an exemplary teacher makes all the difference between good education and bad education. The human factor is the most important and critical in the field of education.

■ Another possibility for the emergence of *Guru-Śiṣya* tradition could have been the necessity for the secure transmission and unadulterated preservation of knowledge. Father-son lineages and teacher-student lineages would have been ideal.

A living Guru is an important factor if education has to be effective, practical and complete.

That is true! The living *Guru* makes sure that knowledge is taught in its purest form and at the same time points out how to apply knowledge in different situations. This kind of teaching of imparting the purest knowledge and skill adapted to the disposition of the student and to the needs of the community can be given only by a living *Guru*. Therefore, I think a living *Guru* is an important factor if education has to be effective, practical and complete.

I myself remember, when I was a student, that teachers made a lot of difference. A teacher who does not take interest in the student as well as in the subject and who does not put his heart and soul into the teaching enterprise will not be able to inspire the student, whereas a committed teacher will be able to leave a mark in the student that will be abiding throughout his life and career.

- Who can be called the ideal *Guru*? Who can be called the ideal *Śiṣya*?

An ideal *Guru* is one who has a complete grasp of his subject. He will be compassionate without selfish motives. He would love his subject and students and will be willing to learn from any source, at any time, and will have a wide range of interests.

An ideal *Śiṣya* is one who has a natural inclination for the subject. He would be ready to sacrifice his immediate gratification needs for the sake of study. He would be fearless and willing to challenge the teacher for the sake of clarity and understanding.

- What is the distinct feature of the style of study in the *Guru-Śiṣya* tradition, if at all it is different from an analytical textual study?

In the ancient *Guru-Śiṣya* tradition, the *Guru* encouraged the student to ask questions. It is only when the student challenges the teacher that he can respond effectively. The method followed is logical analysis, imaginative enquiry, and definition of ultimate goals, daring experiments, and finally personal realisation.

The opinion of authority figures was sought for guidance and inspiration. It is not just accepting authority without questioning. According to Śankarācārya, teaching has to conform to three standards: *śruti*, *yukti* and *anubhava*. *Śruti* is the knowledgebase already available. *Yukti* is analytical thinking based on data. *Anubhava* is one's own personal convictions and experiences.

■ In modern times, the serene atmosphere of the forest, or similar quiet places, conducive to teaching, are hard to find. Is not the place where the teaching takes place important, to make the maximum impact on, and benefit, the student?

It all depends upon the student's background and the type of society in which he lives. The modern student has to discipline his mind so that he can live with the inevitable noise in the society and still learn. A person who has withdrawn to the forest may not feel comfortable in a turbulent society. What is necessary is a learning that is relevant and useful for the community and helpful for the individual's growth. That does not mean that the individual has to sit in the market place and study. He needs a calm and quiet atmosphere whether it is at home, university or library.

I think modern educational institutions generally provide that kind of an atmosphere though there might be the students' own unrest and unruly behaviour.

■ What exactly does the *Guru* try to teach the *Śiṣya*? Are they moral, political, philosophical or spiritual issues?

A *Guru* teaches all these subjects. The *Guru* has to set his spiritual teaching in the moral and political background of the society. Then alone does spirituality become a holistic enterprise. The *Guru* need not teach politics and economics. But he must have a good grasp of these areas of human activity so that when he discusses spiritual and moral issues he is able to contextualise and make it relevant to the individual's daily challenges.

■ One of the *Upaniṣadic* peace invocations prays that let there be no animosity between the teacher and student, and may they nourish each other. What could have been the purpose of such a prayer when it is hard to imagine that there could be negative feelings existing between the teacher and student in the context of sacred teaching and learning?

You are sadly mistaken in thinking that there can be no animosity between a student and teacher. Most of the time, the student takes teaching as an imposition and nobody likes to be imposed upon or told what to do. The teacher may have his own limitations. He can become partial, jealous, irritable and insecure. The student may ask questions which the teacher finds difficult to answer. Also, there can be animosity between students. Therefore it is better not to pretend that everything is fine and all is perfect. It is always good to pray and seek divine help for cultivation of noble values and healthy relationship among the students and between the students and the teacher.

It is always good to pray and seek divine help for cultivation of noble values and healthy relationship among the students and between the students and the teacher.

■ In the context of sects and divisions rampantly occurring, based on differences in detail, in religious and spiritual institutions, how do you think original teachings as well as the binding knot between the *Guru* and *Śiṣya* can be kept intact?

Institutions do not determine the *Guru-Śiṣya* relationship. The *Guru*'s teaching is unconditional. The student is not obligated to work under the umbrella of the teacher and teach exactly the same way that his teacher taught him.

The *Guru-Śiṣya* tradition is not like the hierarchical and institutionalised proselytising church. After the completion of the teaching, the *Guru* asks the student to go out, set up his own establishment and work for the welfare of mankind. The concept of an organisational monolith is originally Western and Christian. The blasphemy, inquisitions, burning at the stake, excommunications are all political in nature.

True spiritual seekers are concerned with knowledge, truth and experience.

In India debate has been, and is, a necessary ingredient of spiritual teaching. India has a long tradition of spiritual debates, and dissent was never misunderstood for creating sects and schools of thought. They were all part of the relentless enquiry into truth, till truth becomes a matter of intimate personal experience.

True, there are sects, divisions and subdivisions in the religious and spiritual institutions in India. But that is only in the lower strata of the society. True spiritual seekers are concerned with knowledge, truth and experience.

■ What is your view on the *Gurukula* system of education, which is being attempted for emulation in some schools now?

I do not think that *Gurukula* system can be revived in the modern context. *Gurukula* system was possible when *Gurus* were the sole repositories of knowledge, societies were far less complex, the pace of change was minimal and the complexity and range of subjects to be taught were almost insignificant. In the modern world no individual can claim mastery over even his chosen field of study. Even values are being customised and we are promoting a million ways of realising God. The old style of a student learning everything from the teacher is simply impossible. The student cannot live such a simplistic lifestyle and come to a very complex and competitive world and still survive. In the modern world, the student has to learn from multiple sources.

What we require is a dialoguing society, where knowledge is available free or at low cost.

What we require is a dialoguing society, where knowledge is available free or at low cost, and responsible students who make use of existing facilities for their education. Let us not try to be nostalgic and romantic about the past. What is necessary is a creative response to the new challenges in the field of education.

■ Are *Guru* and *Śiṣya* cultural role models? Do *Guru* and *Sisya* transcend their roles?

The *Guru* and the *Śiṣya* are not playing roles as such. They are engaged in serious living. The teacher teaches and the student learns. Of course the teacher can be a role model for the student in determining his ideals, values and lifestyles.

But in the modern world the pace of change is so fast that no one person can be a proper role model for any other. All are engaged in creating values that are constantly becoming irrelevant. Hence, in this flux, role models are really roadblocks.

■ What are the best method/s of teaching?

The best method of teaching is teaching only what one has understood and is convinced about. Then alone is communication possible. The teacher must have a learning attitude and an open mind. He must enjoy his teaching. His whole concern should be to help the student understand what he, the teacher, understands. He should not try to impose ideas on his student. He must gently lead the student to discover for himself. The teacher must have the utmost respect for the student and should try to invoke his hidden potentialities. The teacher must never judge or compare the student, nor should he try to teach under the shadow of fear and insecurity.

The ultimate purpose of teaching is to enable the student to respect his deep feelings and individuality and to empower him to take his own decisions and own responsibility for his actions.

The ultimate purpose of teaching is to enable the student to respect his deep feelings and individuality and to empower him to take his own decisions and own responsibility for his actions. The teacher's project is to help the student to discover his true talents and true needs and to train his talents to meet his needs.

- It is increasingly understood that the mindset and receptive nature of students could vary within a group. Also, the same student may not have the same degree of concentration and receptivity at all times. How can the psychological modes and moods of the student be taken care of? Or are they not important enough to be considered?

They are indeed important. In a bad mood the student will not be able to concentrate and comprehend. At the same time the student should not be indulged too much. It is a delicate fine-tuning between positive strokes and necessary tension. If the student is too tense he will not be able to study. If the student is too slack then also he may not study. What is necessary is the right kind of tension conducive to study.

What is necessary is the right kind of tension conducive to study.

- A recent trend noticed in Indian and American societies is the increasing trust accorded by people to saints and *Sanyāsis* to replace the role of psychiatrists and counselors in helping to deal with personal and family conflicts and dilemmas, and also to increase individual work efficiencies. How do you evaluate this trend?

The wisdom tradition that the Sanyāsis and saints represent has a large component of psychological insights in it.

The wisdom tradition that the *Sanyāsi*s and saints represent has a large component of psychological insights in it. Saints and *Swami*s due to their long spiritual practices have strength of character and force of personality whereas the professional psychologists are greedy for money and are entangled in their own personal problems. Saints and *Swamis* are supposedly free from personal and selfish motives. As a result they have better insight into human problems.

Of late, the scientific community, including many psychologists and psychiatrists, has accepted the possibility of soul, spirit or consciousness being a datum influencing and conditioning the processes of the mind and human health. All these might have contributed to the throngs of people you find at *āśrams* and spiritual institutions.

- Is there a possibility of a dialogue between *Guru* and *Śiṣya*? Is it not likely that since teaching is based on authoritative texts and holy scriptures, there could be little room for discussion and exchange?

Any system of teaching that emphasises personal experiences will be unable to proceed without dialogue and discussion. In such a spiritual system personal experience is the ultimate authority. Whether it is Buddhist, Jain or Ḥindu traditions, we find vigorous debates and dialogues amongst students and between students and teachers.

The *Gita* itself is in a dialogical form. Kṛṣṇa's final request to Arjuna was to debate on all the issues in the light of the teaching and decide for himself.

It is the insecure feeling of devotees and the *Guru* that make them cling on to one another. The devotees come to the 'oracle', their *Guru*. The *Guru* obliges them because of his own reasons of insecurity. It is a situation of 'scratch my back and I shall scratch yours.' No self-respecting *Guru* will become a crutch for the student. And no self-confident disciple would want the *Guru* to be a crutch. Even if spiritual knowledge is revelatory and its authority is unimpeachable, it has to be logically analysed and experientially authenticated.

No self-respecting Guru will become a crutch for the student. And no self-confident disciple would want the Guru to be a crutch.

Therefore, in whatever way you look at it, debate and dialogue are the very soul of all teaching.

- Why is *śāstra* (scriptures) the ultimate *pramāṇa* (means of knowledge) in *Vedāntic* traditions?

Śāstra is taken as the ultimate authority because of the nature of the knowledge it deals with. If the knowledge and the reality that the knowledge refers to are subtle and beyond the scope of senses and reasoning which is based on sensate experiences, there is no way that the ordinary individual can dispute the authority of the *śāstra*. This is like the blind man who cannot dispute about the colours in the rainbow simply because he has no means of doing so. What the *śāstra* talks about has to be sympathetically looked into and has to be realised through a programme of discipline, study, reflection and deep meditation.

Debate and dialogue are the very soul of all teaching.

- If *śāstra* is the ultimate authority, it is unlikely that knowledge created by advancements in social, scientific and philosophical studies, would be of any use to the student (or to the teacher) since it denies the possibility of improving or modifying the subject matter and content as dealt with in the *śāstra*!

The study of the *śāstra* deals with subjective self and the holistic nature of reality whereas physical and life sciences, psychology, politics and history deal with tangible interpersonal realities. I do not find any conflict between these disciplines. If a conflict arises between science and *śāstra*, one can solve it intelligently and practically by applying various verification techniques. For example, if the *śāstra* talks about something that is contradictory to observable facts, one can always set aside the *śāstra* and organise one's response according to the observation of science. But if it still does not create the desired result then one can revert to the *śāstra* and organise one's behaviour according to the *śāstra* and see whether that produces the desired result. If both these methods do not work you can exercise your thinking, you can pray and meditate and invoke insights from your deeper self. That is how one can manage one's life by taking the help of various streams of knowledge.

If a conflict arises between science and śāstra, one can solve it intelligently and practically by applying various verification techniques.

■ In olden times, at least as we understand from documents, it is a *Brahmacāri* (celibate) who is eligible for being qualified as a *Śiṣya*. Women and members from other sections of society, like a householder or a warrior, did not have even the remotest possibility of resorting to scriptural study from the *Guru*. But today we see that though the traditional patterns of knowledge transfer are still preserved through orthodox religious and spiritual institutions, more and more women and householders approach spiritual masters and do scriptural studies.

In olden days, *Gurus* accepted only *Brahmacāris*, as resident scholars. They had to live with minimum needs and that too met by the alms they received. The idea was that in this way they could concentrate fully on the study, unencumbered by the thoughts of protecting their possessions. When you have possessions your thinking gets distorted.

Thoughts become possessive and conservative, and impede one's insights and knowledge pursuit. But that did not mean householders, women and lower castes were not allowed into the *āśram* for periodic retreats and reorientation courses. All householders kept contact with *āśrams* and *Guru*s and in times of crisis they always sought and got help from the *Guru*. Anybody was allowed to renounce his household duties, notwithstanding caste or gender status, and join the *āśram* to pursue religious studies single-mindedly. Any such person also would be considered a *Brahmacāri*.

I repeat, nobody was debarred from spiritual studies in ancient India. Only the *paurohityaṃ*, priesthood, were the preserve of a certain class of people, since it was a matter of choice regarding career and living; it did not have anything to do with spiritual practices. That is why a *Purohita*, priest, belongs to one among the four *varnas*, the *Brāhmins*, whereas a saint or a *Swami* belongs to no particular *varṇa* or caste. He belongs to the whole of humanity.

- *Dakṣināmurti* is considered to be the first *Guru* according to a *Vedāntic* prayer. Does this concept have a *Śaivite* influence to its origin? What is the significance of this belief?

Yes, this concept has a *Śaivite* influence because those who pursued knowledge, especially spiritual knowledge, happened to be renunciants. They moved to the Himalayas and worshipped the mountain God *Śiva*. Whereas in the plains the family oriented people, *gṛhasthās*, worshipped *Viṣṇu* and engaged in many rituals.

Knowledge tradition gained a *Śaivite* colour about it and the ritualistic tradition a *Vaiṣṇavite* colour. But there were *Vaiṣṇavite sanyāsis* who traced their knowledge to *Nārayaṇa* himself, which is clear from the invocation *śloka*:

nārāyaṇaṃ padmabhuvaṃ vasiṣtaṃ
śaktiṃ ca tat putraparāśaraṃ ca
vyāsaṃ śukaṃ gaudapādaṃ mahāntaṃ
govinda yogindraṃ athāsya śiṣyaṃ //

śṛiśankarācāryaṃ athāsya padmapādaṃ ca
hastāmalakaṃ ca śiṣyaṃ
taṃ tṛotakaṃ vārtikakāraṃ ca anyān
asmad gurūn santataṃ ānatosmi //

(I salute the succession of Gurus beginning with Nārayaṇa, Brahma, Vasiṣta, Śakti, Parāśara, Vyāsa, Ṣukha, Gaudapāda, Govindapāda, Śankarācārya, Padmapāda,

Hastāmalaka, Totaka, Sureśvarạ Vartikakāṛạ and my present Guru.)

There is also a *Śakti* tradition that traces spiritual knowledge to *Śakti* or *Śārada*, the deity of spiritual knowledge.

■ What is the meaning of *pramāṇa*? Could you also reflect on other philosophical concepts like *prameya* and *pramāta*?

For any experience or knowledge of an object you need these three factors – the object concerned, the subject and the instrument operated by the subject – to contact the object and gain knowledge. These are respectively known as

prameyaṃ – object,

pramāta – subject/knower and

pramāṇaṃ – the means of knowledge.

In objective knowledge, these three factors are absolutely necessary for the creation of knowledge. For example, in the cognition of a pot, the pot is the object. Sense organs and the mind are the instruments, and consciousness conditioned by mind is the knower.

In *Vedāntic* epistemology mind, being subtle, can contact and envelop the object and assume the form of the object like a sensitive film gets the impression of an object. Mind assuming the form of the object, or the impression of the object, is called *vṛtti*, a mode of mind. When the mind contacts a pot and assumes the form of the pot that form is called 'pot-form', *ghata vṛtti*. It is the *vṛtti*, mode of mind, illumined by the conditioned or reflected consciousness that becomes a cognition, *prama*, called *ghata pratyaya*, or 'pot-knowledge'. This experience is presented to the conditioned consciousness and is expressed as 'I see the pot' which is stored in *citta* or memory for future recall. This is called tri-partite knowledge – *tripudi jñāna*.

There is another form of knowledge called self-knowledge where the object is the self. The knowledge of the self is gained by study and reflection on scriptural material. In the case of the self, scripture is the *pramāṇa*. In the case of material objects the sense organs are the *pramāṇa*.

■ *Upaniṣadic* literature is marked by beautiful and thought provoking stories narrated by the *Ṛṣi/Guru* and simple experiments engaged in by the student as directed by them. What is the significance of these stories and apparently simple experiments (for example the illustration of '*nyagrōdha*' seed in the *Cāndōgya Upaniṣad*) detailed in these texts, which represent more of a narrative influenced by folk psychology?

Stories have a great value in spiritual teaching, invoking the imaginative powers of the students.

To convey subtle ideas, words are often insufficient and incompetent. The mind needs the aid of metaphors, myths and stories. Even Einstein used stories and metaphors to explain the relativity theory to his audience.

In the spiritual field, with the help of metaphors, folk tales, and stories the mind can be elevated to higher levels of energies and understanding. Such stories have a great value in spiritual teaching, invoking the imaginative powers of the students.

For example, when we say that consciousness is like the ocean, blue sky, space or the mountaintop, you get an idea of the vastness, boundlessness, the immaculateness and stillness of the self. Or, in the context of discrimination, *viveka*, the metaphor used is 'lotus in a pond'. This imagery is so complete that no more words are necessary to describe it. So too, to describe a still mind, the example of a 'non-flickering flame' is given.

Simple experiments have universal validity and go deep into one's heart. It does not provoke doubts and apprehensions and fill the blanks left by verbal descriptions. They are more direct and nonverbal. The test of a method of teaching is its architectural simplicity and verbal parsimony. That is what we find in the *Upaniṣadic* teaching.

Simple experiments have universal validity.

Whenever one explains subtle ideas, which cannot be objectively identified and demonstrated, metaphors become handy and useful. Sometimes great teachers use a series of metaphors, parables, anecdotes and stories to create a subtle sequence of logic and create still subtler insights. Therefore I think spiritual traditions like *Vedānta* use logic, statements of great masters, metaphors and anecdotes and inspiring statements to create the vision that the teacher wants to communicate.

- Is there a difference between the style and mode of teaching and the teacher-taught roles as portrayed in the *Bhagavad Gītā* and the *Upaniṣadic* literature?

There is a difference in the context of the teaching though not in the message. The renunciant teachers taught the

Upaniṣads to renunciant students in the sylvan and silent valleys of Himalayas. The language was direct and simple. No attempt was made to persuade the student to follow the teaching. The teacher did not motivate the student to engage in anything.

The *Bhagavad Gītā*, on the contrary, was taught in the din and roar of the battlefield. The student was a man of action who did not like the word 'defeat' and there was the great charming personality of the teacher, Lord Kṛṣṇa, worldly-wise and spiritually detached. The setting of the *Gītā* is grand and dramatic and the character of the student is very complex. The personality of the teacher is so complete and the crisis of the moment so grave with such depth and width and practical relevance, that no other teaching can match the sublime *Bhagavad Gītā*.

The personality of the teacher is so complete and the crisis of the moments so grave the teaching gained such depth and width and practical relevance that no teaching can match the sublime Bhagavad Gītā.

If the *Upaniṣadic* setting and teaching can be compared to a seed, I would compare the setting and teaching of the *Gītā* to a fully-grown tree with foliage, flowers and fruits, with its leaves swaying in the wind and shining in the sunlight. The *Gītā* is truly the natural culmination of the *Upaniṣad*s.

- The *Dakṣiṇāmurti Stōtraṃ* gives the romantic picture, though metaphorically, of the young *Guru* and the old *Śiṣyās*. But much of the *Upaniṣadic* literature portrays *Gurus* who are not only old, but married and with children!

Both backgrounds are relevant, each in their own way. *Upaniṣadic Ṛṣi*s were very experienced, old, wise and withdrawn from the noisy world while the students were young, inexperienced and with dreams in their heart, fire in their belly, and stars in their eyes. It was the meeting of rich experience with raw energy.

The other side of the picture is suggested by the imagery of the *Dakṣiṇāmurti Stotraṃ* – of the young teacher sitting under the banyan tree surrounded by gray and wrinkled faces burdened by the past and lost in memories. The *Guru* because of his spiritual enlightenment is healthy, dynamic, young and ever fresh. He has discovered himself to be the unborn, undying spirit, whereas the students identified with the body and mind have become old and tired, burdened with the memories of the past and the illnesses of the body.

These two pictures are relevant in understanding the dynamics between the *Guru* and the disciples, the *Guru*'s wisdom and youth, and the disciples' old age and stupidities, and the possibility of deliverance.

- The student, according to the guidelines prescribed for traditional *Śiṣyās*, has to serve the *Guru* and his household for an indefinite period of time, until the *Guru* feels that the *Śiṣya* is ready for the teaching. What is the meaning of these psychological manipulations and physical exercises in the context of sacred and serious teaching and learning?

It is for the *Guru* to understand the psychological profile of the student so that he can give necessary instructions to rectify the student's defects and organise the student's mind for the purpose of study. The student has to go through various situations to understand his own mind, to purify it, which will not be possible without facing the puzzles and contradictions and paradoxes of the world. It gives the student an opportunity to learn from the bottom up, or 'to learn hands on'. A serious and determined student will take all these manipulations as learning processes. If the teacher tries to dominate and dictate and psychologically break down the student for his own egoistic pleasures that will not serve the purpose.

I do admit that there is much in the old system that is nothing but psychological manipulation for dominance and control. But the teacher who is a master of the subject will have no need to manipulate his student. His only passion will be to share his vision with his student.

■ What is your advice for the aspirant of *brahmavidya*, the sacred knowledge of one's Self?

The aspirant of *brahmavidya* must relentlessly question, reflect and be honest about his motives while he interacts with the world and pursues his desired projects. That would help him harmonise his motives, thoughts, deeds and relationships. Such an integrated mind would get access to the infinite spirit that is *Brahman*. In this effort he takes the help of *Guru*s and scriptures, Gods and parents, and his own self.

■ How do you see yourself as a teacher, a counsellor or a *Sanyāsi*?

I enjoy all these roles and it is my way of exploring and expressing myself. What I enjoy, I am sure others also will enjoy. That is the only test of whether you are going along the right path – do you enjoy what you do?

9

The Bhagavad Gītā and the Battlefield of Life

■ Can there really be a discussion relating a text that was supposedly written 5000 years ago and modern life situations which are in totally different sociocultural conditions, and therefore marked by different and complex psychological states?

Though the external conditions of life change, the psychological conditions remain the same. It is the state of mind that affects our evaluation of life's challenges and our responses to those challenges. The mind operates under the same emotions, like fear, jealousy, greed, anger, anxiety and attachment to the results of our actions. Anxiety about the results of actions creates a whole lot of psychological problems that affect our health and quality of life. The human problem will remain essentially the same even if the external circumstances change.

Men and women who lived 5000 years ago and those living today engage in almost the same kinds of activities. They eat, sleep, reproduce, fight for territory, money and power, and domination of others. I do not find any great change in human psychology though the material environment has changed drastically. Quarrels have always been there amongst people for property, which includes women, slaves and animals as in the old days. As long as private property and man's insecurity remain so long his psychological problems will also remain.

As long as private property and man's insecurity remain so long his psychological problems will also remain.

Hence there is great relevance for an ancient text that deals with fundamental human problems and man's search for answers. Humankind can draw great insights from ancient texts in understanding and offering solutions to contemporary problems.

- Why do you think the *Bhagavad Gītā*, its background set in the specific context of a battlefield, has a universal reference to different life situations?

All life situations involve choice making between right and wrong, between immediate gratification and deeper and sustainable satisfaction, between that which is lasting and that which is fleeting etc. Man's economic life also involves moment-to-moment choices. The modern market place is a veritable battlefield. Businessmen try to expand their market shares, acquire new markets, edge out rivals' products, and reign supreme.

I find that the battlefield background of the *Bhagavad Gītā* has an enduring appeal and much relevance for modern man who faces life as many challenges of choice making. The *Bhagavad Gītā*'s predecessors, the *Upaniṣads*, were composed in the silent valleys of the Himalayas whereas Vyāsa composed the *Gītā* and placed it in the midst of the *Mahābhārata*, the story of war between two royal families.

■ What is the central message of the *Gītā*?

Different scholars and devotees of the *Gītā* give different ideals as the central message of the *Gītā*. Some say that the *Gītā* teaches active resistance to evil. Some others say that the *Gītā*'s message is unflinching commitment to one's duty, to family and society. Yet others say that it is an impassioned exhortation to renounce the fruits of one's works. According to some the central message of the *Gītā* is immortality of self and unity of life.

According to me, the main teaching of the *Gītā* is to make work and relationships a means of self-exploration and self-expression.

■ To compare or situate life within a battlefield, metaphorically to begin with, sounds rather sadistic and more fearful than pleasant.

Unfortunately life is situated in unpleasant and uncomfortable environs. We find death, disease and the strong exploiting the weak as a sort of common experience in daily life.

True scripture has to show us the path from where we are now to where we want to reach.

True scripture has to show us the path from where we are now to where we want to reach. There is no point in simply building castles in the air. It is essentially a question of keeping one's balance and poise, and doing the right thing in a turbulent, violent and nasty world.

By situating the *Gītā* in the din and roar of the battlefield the author of the *Gītā* makes a statement that life is a battlefield, but human ingenuity and creativity can make it a playing field for self-discovery. Here you find the marriage of life's realities and life's dreams. I think it is unique to set the spiritual teaching in the situation of a battlefield.

- Why does the text begin with an appraisal of the two arrays of armies in the Kurukṣetra battlefield rather than getting into the spiritual teachings offered by Lord Kṛṣṇa to Arjuna?

It is to reflect on the practical human situation and also the psychological realities of human life. The psyche of man is portrayed as a battlefield between conflicting desires and deeds. As they say there is a lower man and a higher man, or the pleasure principle and death wish, the conscious and unconscious, god and devil.

The psyche of man is portrayed as a battlefield between conflicting desires and deeds.

Human mind is capable of imagining the opposite of any proposition. Hence it is basically dialectical. Maybe as the philosopher Hegel said, life unfolds in terms of dialectics of thesis and antithesis resolving in a synthesis. By opening the text with the description of a battlefield with two armies facing each other the author tries to describe the human psyche and the conflicts that man undergoes in daily life. The blind king represents the limited egoistic human being who is always anxious about the outcome of his work and his future. The two armies

Human mind is capable of imagining the opposite of any proposition.

Hence it is basically dialectical.

represent opposing forces, those of good and evil, positive and negative, integrative and dissipative. The battlefield represents this complex life of mankind where he struggles between opposing forces. His insecurity and anxieties are all described in the opening chapter of the *Bhagavad Gītā*.

- Why do you think the Kurukṣetra battlefield was taken as the opportunity for Lord Kṛṣṇa to teach Arjuna the most profound and complex spiritual truths, and not any of the earlier more relaxed situations when they were together?

We ask fundamental questions when we face great crises in life. Our mind becomes acute, intellect sharp and energies harnessed. Our ability to take risks and pursue unconventional ideas is greater in such crises. In a relaxed situation we are not challenged sufficiently to bring out our best, or to ask fundamental questions, or seek unconventional answers.

To provoke the human, to ask deeper questions one needs a deep crisis of values.

To provoke the individual to ask deeper questions one needs a deep crisis of values. That is what we find in the very beginning of the *Bhagavad Gītā* where the protagonist Arjuna seeks answers for fundamental questions, dissatisfied with partial answers and solutions. Instead of thinking of himself as belonging to a particular party he thinks as a representative of the whole of humanity. He does not ask victory for himself but he wants victory for righteousness. He wants to know the truth.

The most profound truth can be appreciated and understood only when our life is at great stake and we are on the verge of losing everything. It was appropriate then on the part of Lord Kṛṣṇa to expound the greatest truth to Arjuna whose value systems collapsed completely and who could see the hollowness of the ordinary ends that he was pursuing and the parochial value systems that he was upholding.

The most profound truth can be appreciated and understood only when our life is at great stake and we are on the verge of losing everything.

■ Why is Arjuna's *viṣāda* (sorrow) called *yoga* (union)?

As I said earlier, sorrow arises when man finds himself in a dilemma. You are not able to find solutions to problems and you also find that all solutions are equally unacceptable. In such a situation man becomes sad. He finds his opponents and his detractors are all victims of situations and are moved by some power beyond their control. There is nobody to blame for the human condition and there is nobody above blame.

When he finds that all heroes collapse like castles on sand, a sensitive individual becomes sad which makes him reflect fundamentally on the human condition and seek radical solutions.

■ What is the central cause of depression?

The central cause of depression is lack of growth, and lack of opportunities to express one's energies.

The central cause of depression is lack of growth, and lack of opportunities to express one's energies. There can be explanations like the chemistry of body, position of planets, lack of appreciation or love etc. But the main cause of depression is the lack of opportunity to learn and grow. The individual requires lifelong training to make use of opportunities positively. One cannot overnight become a learning and a growing individual. It requires goals beyond one's little self, goals that are accommodative rather than exclusivistic. A person who is self-confident and self-motivated and sees himself as the source of energy and values will never be depressed. He is always able to place events and experiences in a positive orientation and be ready for any challenge and situation.

■ When a person breaks down owing to depression and is confused about making choices or decisions, an appropriate possibility, from a counselor's point of view would be to allow him to view the situation in its entirety. Is it not unlikely that the counselor would present him with lofty spiritual ideas about an eternal self, liberation and such metaphysical and non-existential issues?

In fact Lord Kṛṣṇa allowed Arjuna to express himself unconditionally and explore various scenarios that the battle projected. At the end Arjuna, caught in the contradictions in his own arguments and reasoning, thoroughly confused, sat quiet. Then alone did Lord Kṛṣṇa begin his teaching.

Lord Kṛṣṇa presented many scenarios for Arjuna's consideration: from the standpoint of eternal self that nothing fundamentally happens in this world; from the standpoint of the fleeting world that there is nothing which exists permanently in this world; from the standpoint of human duties and responsibilities, that is not withstanding what, a human being has innate duties; from the standpoint of the all-pervading god who has to be obeyed and served unconditionally; from the standpoint of a global achiever who focuses on work and organises his energies dispassionately pursuing excellence.

From all these standpoints the response to the immediate crisis happened to be the same, to engage in the immanent battle without regard to the consequences. Life has a moment-to-moment immediacy that requires spontaneous response.

Life has a moment-to-moment immediacy that requires spontaneous response.

A prolonged deliberation that delays action is suicidal and life denying, though impulsive action without due deliberation is foolish and fatal. If one is forced to make a choice between action and deliberation the *Gītā* recommends action over deliberation. If you miss action, then deliberation becomes fruitless and meaningless. But if you engage in action, lack of deliberation can always be rectified from learning opportunities.

Lord Kṛṣṇa does not teach any lofty ideal in an unrelated sense that you imply.

Lord Kṛṣṇa's teaching is very practical: act and learn, not learn and act. Learning is always through activity.

- There is a verse in the second chapter which says "existence never becomes non-existence, and non-existence will never have a chance to exist". What does this statement mean?

It means that nothing actually ever changes. What IS is and what IS NOT is not. Nothing is ever created. Nothing is ever destroyed. This has an echo from the scientific law of conservation of matter. It is the vision of the wise that what is created and what is destroyed is nonexistent. What exists is not subject to creation and destruction.

I think that this statement of the *Gītā* is one of the wisest sayings and one who can contemplate on the beginning and end of things, understands that nothing begins or ends. Life is one whole. This insight makes man wise and stable, enables him to go through the turbulence and drama of life without losing his balance and moorings.

- Desire is the promoting force of activity. How can one renounce desire and still be active?

As far as I can see desire is the instrument for self-exploration and self-expression. Ordinarily desire is to possess something that exists outside oneself and to indulge. Such desires arise from self-ignorance and sense of inadequacy. Such desires constrict and are the cause of human sorrow and suffering.

There are desires that arise from self-knowledge, and from an urge to share, to experiment, to question and to seek truth. Such desires are liberating.

There are two types of desires: desire to have and indulge, and the desire to share and grow. By changing the direction of desire one is able to transform desire energy from a dissipative to an integrative experience.

- To be active and participating in life situations involves the perpetuation of the socio-cultural physical self. To abide in the spiritual self involves contemplation and self-enquiry. How can activity (*karma*) and contemplation (*ātma vicāra*) go together?

This question arises from the dualistic concept that the *atman*, the self, is divorced from mind, body and nature. Cultural and social institutions are all creations of mind. They are not opposed to the self just as the hub of a wheel is not opposed to the spokes and rim of the wheel. In my vision the self is a composite of spirit, feelings, thoughts, sensations and environment.

Contemplation of the self is abiding in, or living as the self.

It need not go against social and mental activities.

Contemplation of the self is abiding in, or living as the self. It need not go against social and mental activities. In fact it is only when we act that there is thinking. Thinking is an energy that expresses the self. The notion that contemplation is opposed to activity is due to lack of practice. In fact true activity is true contemplation. Contemplation is experiencing oneself deeply, comprehensively and abundantly. It is not remaining idle and aloof from all activities. That is the teaching of the great scriptures, the experience of great masters. That is the need of our times, to understand activity as the greatest contemplation.

- You said that self is a composite of sensations, ideas, individual identity feelings and environment. If so, is the individual self nothing more than a materialistic construct which can also be analysed into parts and reconstructed?

I do not believe that anything can be understood by dividing it into individual parts. To know a part is to know the whole. When I say that the individual is a composite, I do not mean he is a product of various constituent factors.

> ***No kind of objective investigation and studies can fully comprehend the actual individual.***
>
> ***That is why I think that experience is the ultimate and not knowledge.***

What I mean is that the individual is not an isolated entity distinct from other entities. The individual is a whole person. In that wholeness there are variable and invariable factors and only the individual can experience himself totally. No kind of objective investigation and studies can fully comprehend the actual individual.

That is why I think that experience is the ultimate and not knowledge. Knowledge of the neural processes that describe love is not the actual experience of love. The lover alone can know the sweetness of love.

■ The physical, social and mental worlds are not products of my creation. They have their own existences. Even when renunciation is done, whether it is of the untrue idea of non-self (*anātman*), expectation of comfortable and appealing results, negative emotions like fear, greed, lust arise, since they belong to the world which I haven't created. How can renunciation be possible unless it be just theoretical and a belief?

The idea of renunciation is not to get away from either the desirable or the undesirable, but to expand and include, to associate and incorporate, to find a place for all that falls in the scope of one's awareness. That is possible only by withdrawing one's extreme obsession with limited objects, and seeing the object of one's desire or obsession in the context of all other objects.

I would understand renunciation as an attitude of inclusiveness rather than exclusiveness, an ability to embrace more and more than a withdrawal from what is unpleasant and inconvenient. From that standpoint self becomes consciousness that is all-inclusive, and renunciation is expansion and engagement rather than contraction and disengagement. Renunciation is pouring out one's infinite spiritual energy rather than curling up in a remote cave, or getting lost in an impossible idea of withdrawal from the world. As one's mind expands and integrates with the world the so-called negative emotions – like fear, greed, jealousy and anger – will lose their sting. Positive attitudes like love, care, and healthy respect for others will naturally arise.

- Realisation of myself as *sacchidānanda ātman* entails my transcending dualities, the primary ones being those of space (existence and non-existence) and time (past, present and future). With the transcendence of time and space, the essential structures for experiencing and expressing the physical, emotional and social self, become unavailable. Once the experience is within and extended by spatiotemporal events, then I am again in the world of duality, of birth and death, and experiences limited by them.

Transcending time and space does not mean separating from time and space.

Transcending time and space does not mean separating from time and space. It only means that instead of being an event in time and space you reduce time and space into an event in your awareness. It is only then the self-realised individual is able to use time and space and its various structures as a conduit for expressing the infinite self.

Dualistic reasoning causes the notion that realisation is elimination of time and space or separating oneself from time-space. Hence Śankara defines time and space as *anirvacaniya*, indescribable. He does not categorise them as existence or nonexistence, past or future. He calls them phenomena which defy categorisation, but which have existence as instrumentalities. By themselves they are not meaningful or self-existent. But they come into existence in the context of self or consciousness. I would call time-space the expressions, or the primary extension, of the self.

■ What am I really capable of renouncing? What am I really capable of acquiring?

Nothing. You can acquire only that which you do not have. You can renounce only that which is other than you. In the strict sense, renunciation is not possible. Only enunciation is possible, that 'I am in all, all are in me. I *am* all'.

Having said this, one can say that renunciation is expressing yourself, your full potential. Acquisition is of all those mental qualities and disciplines that will enable such renunciation.

■ The *Gītā* talks about *sthitaprajña*, *yogi*, *guṇātita*, *kṣetrajña*, *sanyāsi*, *jñāni* etc. Are these descriptions of the same state of mind/self or have they different implications?

They indicate the same state of consciousness. They are descriptions from different standpoints. *Sthitaprajña* means one who has clear knowledge about himself that is not shaken by experiences. *Sanyāsi* means one who has renounced notions about himself which are based on physical experiences, and has come to the true understanding of his enduring self. *Guṇātita* means one who is no more a plaything of the *guṇās* or influenced by the *guṇās*; but uses *guṇās* for self-expression. *Jñāni* is one who has abiding self-knowledge. *Kṣetrajña* is one who is the observer of the field of change and *Yogi* is one who experiences the unity of existence. They are all different words and descriptions indicating the same reality and accomplishment.

■ If I am *sacchidānanda ātma*, why is my immediate feeling that of a limited self and not otherwise?

The answer is implied in the question, that you are not what you feel. In other words, what you feel is a limited expression of yourself. Your feeling does not exhaustively describe your identity. Just as a mirror is not conditioned by what it reflects so, too, your consciousness is not limited by what you feel. On reflection you understand that it is your choice to feel limited or limitless but your being is uninfluenced by what you feel or what you have.

Objectification is an inevitable process in the self-discovery of the subject.

This question is answered in terms of 'ignorance' by the scriptures. Because of our obsession with what we feel, see and have, we become oblivious of what we *are*. But the restlessness involved in that self-alienation compels a movement towards self-search and final realisation. Objectification is necessary for a deepened understanding of the subject. Subject without the object is dull and homogeneous and its infinite potentialities remain unrevealed. Objectification is an inevitable process in the self-discovery of the subject.

■ In the twelfth chapter Lord Kṛṣṇa says "renounce all activities unto me, and worship me alone by *ananya yoga*". This statement primarily would mean dedication unto and liberation through a personal god. Is there more than theology in this pronouncement?

Lord Kṛṣṇa introduces himself in the *Gītā* as the universal consciousness in which everything exists, from which everything manifests and unto which everything returns. In a very revealing verse in the ninth chapter he describes himself to be the invisible consciousness that pervades the manifest world, who lives in every unique expression in the world but at the same time is free from the limitation and contingency of the world. In the eleventh chapter he presents himself as the totality of manifestations – he is the mountains, rivers, stars, and he is even the infinitesimal speck of dust that is trampled under your feet. He also describes himself as the experiencing consciousness in every individual.

A symbol should never be confused with what is symbolised.

From this standpoint, to surrender to Lord Kṛṣṇa does not mean surrendering to an individual god but living in close contact with universal intelligence and drawing one's energy from that imperishable source. It is only in one context in the *Gītā* that Lord Kṛṣṇa describes himself to be a person with four hands and a face, in the anthropomorphic form. That is only to console Arjuna and help him remember the all-pervading God.

A symbol should never be confused with what is symbolised.

■ If Lord Kṛṣṇa is the mountains, rivers, and the entirety of existence, including the speck of dust, how can I dedicate myself to this and take refuge in this kind of a personality or totality of natural forces and existences?

Devotion is a process of feeling empathy and relatedness to the world. Physically and mentally we are all part of the world process. The food that you eat which sustains your thought is produced by the plants, which themselves are the result of a certain energy level that exists as the interaction between the earth and the sun. It is sunlight converted to tissues by a process of photosynthesis that becomes food. So too, thoughts and feelings are influenced by your environment and people around you. Realising that you are part of the visible world as a body-mind being is the meaning of surrender to Lord Kṛṣṇa.

When that integration happens, which is otherwise called *samatva buddhi* or balanced mind, you will be able to experience the spiritual ground of everything. Since the whole of existence is alive and intelligent, integration is not a mechanical process but a feelingfull, experiential realisation.

■ How would you look at the personality of Lord Kṛṣṇa and Arjuna?

Lord Kṛṣṇa represents the invisible spirit that is the ground of the manifested world. He is also the lifespring in living beings. He is the eternal motivator and inspirer of humankind. Arjuna represents the man of action who is ready to take up any challenge that comes his way. He is a warrior who is determined to win and enjoy his victory. The union of these two spirits, the active and personalised and the contemplative and universal, ensures lasting victory, human excellence and social justice.

The union of these two spirits, the active and personalised and the contemplative and universal, ensures lasting victory, human excellence and social justice.

■ How would I be able to know what is best for me in a given situation? What should be the guiding principles when I am faced with situations which offer me many equally valid choices to make?

You have to ask your own inner voice that is a function of your education, your value system, your aspirations, your fears and your needs that define your uniqueness. It does not mean that your inner voice will not give you uncertain or confused answers because of which you may be hesitant, self-doubting and fumbling. But your inner voice has an innate sense of what is good for you and the light that it sheds will be almost true to your destiny. The sure path shown by others will make you mechanical and insipid and you will never learn nor grow by that route. You may listen to other authorities but, ultimately, you have to be responsible for your choices and be a light unto yourself.

■ Is realisation an event in time? Is self-ignorance an event in time?

Realisation is not an event in time. It is an understanding of all events as ephemeral and transient. Ignorance is time and time is an event in consciousness. There are endless series of events creating the experience of past, present and future. Realisation is the knowledge that the spirit of the experiencer is not displaced by events and experiences. Realisation is a non-event and not one among the events.

Realisation is a non-event and not one among the events.

- In the eighteenth chapter Lord Kṛṣṇa makes a promise that if all *dharma* is renounced unto him, and he alone is taken as the refuge, all the sins of that person will be taken by the Lord, and he will be granted *mokṣa*. What is the secondary meaning of this verse other than the apparent religious meaning?

I do not consider the religious meaning separate from the implied or secondary meaning. I see only one meaning, that one should not define oneself by the actions and consequences of one's actions. One's infinitude and identity is not the sum total of one's actions and their results.

The spirit is a-historical non-local and a-temporal but at the same time is the essence of all manifestations.

The spirit is a-historical non-local and a-temporal but at the same time is the essence of all manifestations.

When Lord Kṛṣṇa asks you to renounce all actions, good and bad, and come to him, what he means is to be a responsible choice maker, a master of work and express your infinite potential through the moment-to-moment choices you make.

■ If I renounce my sense of self which is limited/ extended by causal events and time–space duality, I can at the most be imagining that I am a 'universal self'; or by constant thought of that kind, guide the brain to offer me visions and out-of-self experiences. Is the renunciation of the sense of self really possible? If you say that renunciation of self only means extending my emotions and sensitivities to the entire living and non-living world that becomes a psychological activity founded on moral principles. How can it be called a spiritual state of being?

Renunciation of the self is a philosophically ambiguous term. What Buddhists mean by renunciation of self is the renunciation of all ideas of self and to remain free from conclusions. When Hindu thinkers use the word renunciation, it is the renunciation of ego and realisation of true self. Realisation of self concomitantly means relating to the world of events and things in a loving mode.

To love means to respect the uniqueness of the other and accommodate him/her in the lover's consciousness. It is not a moral principle or a mandatory value imposed upon the lover. It is a spontaneous experience of the realised person. I do not use the word love in the ordinary sense of attaching to somebody with personal expectations or clinging on to somebody because of the aroused libido or insecure feelings. Love is a state of awareness where there is a healthy and honest interaction with others.

The idea of renouncing the self and detailed explanations of the renunciant's state of mind could work on the brain and create imaginary experiences. Or it can actually lead to enlightenment if those experiences are further questioned against one's understanding of the self. In spiritual realisation this problem is envisaged as to whether the brain creates imaginary false experiences or the brain only invokes and reports the reality. At this moment I remember Gaudapāda's advice, that is, not to cling on to any kind of experience in the path to self-realisation.

Self-experience is not an objective experience that appears as an event but a holistic experience that does not lapse into memory and get displaced by any other experience.

What is spontaneous in a realised person becomes an imposed value system for historians and academicians.

Spiritual masters have already envisaged your objections and apprehensions. They already have forewarned against imagined and mimicked experiences. What is spontaneous in a realised person becomes an imposed value system for historians and academicians. Ultimately what happens is the experience of a consciousness that is accommodative and expressive of its potential. That is the realisation of self.

■ What is your appraisal of Vyāsa, the author of *Bhagavad Gītā*?

I consider Vyāsa to be the most authentic representative of Hinduism and the Indian culture. His interests are wholesome and include all aspects of human life: spiritual, moral, cultural, economic, political. There is no field of human endeavour that he has not touched and enriched. From that reckoning Buddha and Śankarācārya seem to be half-developed individuals creating the impression that there is nothing more to life than an emaciated spiritual life. The wholeness that we see in Vyāsa is missing in Śankararācārya and Buddha though their contributions to humanity are very profound.

■ What is *bhūtaprakṛtimokṣaṃ*?

Prakṛti means the material and mental world that are described as *bhūta,* meaning, that which appears and disappears. That which appears and disappears has no existence by itself. It is only a shadow of something that is everlasting. When you see a shadow your attention is drawn to the real and the shadow is then not counted or is ignored. We call it *mokṣa* or *abhāva darśana* or seeing the absence of shadow.

To put it briefly, when you experience the world and thoughts, instead of giving reality to the experience and thoughts and getting focused and lost in that flux, every experience reminds you of the self. This moment-to-moment experience leads you to the self and confirms and deepens your self-realisation, a state where the world and worldly experiences instead of distracting you gives you deepened self-abidance. Worldly experiences become spiritual experiences. That is the meaning of *bhūtaprakrtimokṣaṃ* that the Lord describes in the last *śloka* of the thirteenth chapter of the *Bhagavad Gītā*.